# Understanding Your Three-Year-Old

## *Louise Emanuel*

Jessica Kingsley Publishers
London and Philadelphia

First published in 2005
by Jessica Kingsley Publishers
116 Pentonville Road
London N1 9JB, UK
and
400 Market Street, Suite 400
Philadelphia, PA 19106, USA

*www.jkp.com*

**Library of Congress Cataloging in Publication Data**
Emanuel, Louise, 1953-
    Understanding your three-year-old / Louise Emanuel.
        p. cm. -- (Understanding your child series)
    Includes bibliographical references and index.
    ISBN 1-84310-243-9 (pbk.)
    1. Toddlers. 2. Child rearing. I. Title. II. Series.
    HQ774.5.E48 2004
    305.233--dc22

                                                2004012454


**British Library Cataloguing in Publication Data**
A CIP catalogue record for this book is available from the British Library

ISBN 978 1 84310 243 4


Printed and Bound in Great Britain by
Athenaeum Press, Gateshead, Tyne and Wear

# Contents

# Foreword

The Tavistock Clinic has an international reputation as a centre of excellence for training, clinical mental health work, research and scholarship. Established in 1920, its history is one of groundbreaking work. The original aim of the Clinic was to offer treatment which could be used as the basis of research into the social prevention and treatment of mental health problems, and to teach these emerging skills to other professionals. Later work turned towards the treatment of trauma, the understanding of conscious and unconscious processes in groups, as well as important and influential work in developmental psychology. Work in perinatal bereavement led to a new understanding within the medical profession of the experience of stillbirth, and of the development of new forms of support for mourning parents and families. The development in the 1950s and 1960s of a systemic model of psychotherapy, focusing on the interaction between children and parents and within families, has grown into the substantial body of theoretical knowledge and therapeutic techniques used in the Tavistock's training and research in family therapy.

The Understanding Your Child series has an important place in the history of the Tavistock Clinic. It has been issued in completely new form three times: in the 1960s, the 1990s, and in 2004. Each time the authors, drawing on their clinical background and specialist training, have set out to reflect on the extraordinary story of 'ordinary development' as it was observed and experienced at the time. Society changes, of course, and so has this series, as it attempts to make sense of everyday accounts of the ways in which a developing child interacts with his or her parents, carers and the wider world. But within this changing scene there has been something constant, and it is best described as a continuing enthusiasm for a view of

7

development which recognizes the importance of the strong feelings and emotions experienced at each stage of development.

This book continues the complex story of development, already unfolding in a dramatic way in the first three volumes of this series. This book, although it can be read on its own, will be put in context by the world of the baby, the one-year-old, and the two-year-old. It is becoming clear that new developments are linked in subtle ways to earlier versions of themselves. There are moments too (beautifully described by Louise Emanuel) when three-year-olds abandon the strain of being three by reverting to a baby state, or alternatively a "mini- adult" state. This is not the whole story however. Inexorably, change happens. The expanding social life of the three-year-old – imaginative play, a deepening emotional life, and, in short, the emergence of a clearer sense of identity – are described in a thoughtful and engaging way.

*Jonathan Bradley*
*Child Psychotherapist*
*General Editor of the Understanding Your Child series*

# Acknowledgements

Many thanks to the following for their contributions of ideas and material to this book:

Michal Gurion for some of the material about 'Penny' in Chapter 2 (which will appear in a book to be published in 2005).

Lizzie Overton, James and Ruben Greyson for thoughts about 'Max'.

Paolo Carignani, Holly Dwyer, Susan Reid, Judith Trowell, Alison Cantle and Margaret Rustin.

# Introduction

A.A. Milne's character Christopher Robin, looking back from the ripe old age of six, talks of hardly being "me" at three. But anyone who spends time with three-year-olds can see how quickly their minds, bodies and personalities are developing. Each day they seem to become more articulate, competent, imaginative and challenging. It is in this fourth year that the young child really establishes his identity. This is me! (I will use "he" and "she" in alternate chapters when referring to children of either gender.)

The "nearly three" and the "rising four"-year-old are separated by a year of incredibly rich experience and development, during which many changes and transitions take place. By three a child will be spending at least some time in alternative childcare as many parents will have returned to work, and he will usually start going to nursery school during this year. This is a big event, and expectations of the three-year-old rise, as he is seen to be leaving babyhood and toddler-hood behind him.

But is he really so big and grown-up? He may appear to be competent and in control at times, especially when he is in familiar surroundings and having his needs thoughtfully attended to (he may be able to switch on the video player without help and already have some computer skills). He may even become quite bossy and tyrannical, ordering his parents or siblings around. Ben refused to let his parents call him "Benny" when he turned three, saying, "I'm a big boy now, and I'm in charge!"

Yet there is another side to the three-year-old, much younger and more baby-like, that shows itself surprisingly often. He may busy himself pretending to "sort out Daddy's papers in his office" at one moment, and ask for a nappy to poo in the next. He may be "good as gold" at nursery, then come home grumpy and tired, at last able to let down his guard and show the strain he has been under. He may just curl up on your lap and suck his thumb or ask for a bottle.

A parent told me she thought her three-year-old and 14-year-old daughters resembled each other a great deal: defiant/rebellious, curious/exploratory, risk-taking, pushing the boundaries at every opportunity, needy and dependent one minute, fiercely independent the next. These two developmental phases have much in common. In particular, they are both characterized by surges of emotional intensity, feelings that often quickly bubble up to the surface and erupt into tantrums, sudden collapses into tears, or controlling bossiness. As a parent it is often tricky to strike the right balance between not expecting too much of a three-year-old who is still just leaving toddler-hood, and also ensuring that he is given enough opportunities to expand.

## Developing skills and strong wills

The child's social world expands during this year as he generally becomes more able to play together with his peers at nursery or at home, enjoying imaginary games and role-play. Parents still need to be close by to supervise, as feelings can run high when it comes to sharing, choosing play partners or waiting for turns.

The three-year-old delights in his physical capacities and enjoys outdoor activities. He can run confidently, and is beginning to skip, hop and ride a trike. He may have started taking swimming or toddler gymnastics classes. He enjoys painting, simple crafts, puzzles and matching games, but is still fond of a few special "baby" toys. His ability to play creatively and imaginatively on his own and with others is increasing, as is his love of language. By three a child enjoys having conversations, has learnt to ask "Why?" and will use it endlessly. His speech continues to develop as he makes up new words, and uses those he has heard spoken, sometimes amusingly out of context. Three-year-old Jenny, whose older brother had recently been revising for his science test, was taken swimming and feeling the cold water whined, "Daddy do I really have to swim in this $H_2O$?" Rose, picking up on some harmless banter over the weekend, told her nursery teacher, "My mother's an alcoholic!" when in fact her mother drank the odd glass of wine or beer, no more.

Individual tastes, likes and dislikes, and eccentricities will become even more established, and these may not always conform to society's norms. Dot was given a frilly rainbow petticoat for her birthday and insisted on wearing it to nursery on *top* of her dress for a whole week. Her mother decided this was a battle of wills not worth engaging in. Gavin and his family were about to go for a walk before their picnic lunch when he spied a bottle of pickled cucumbers of which he was particularly fond. When told he could have one at lunchtime he said nothing but while the others were getting ready he sneaked back to the picnic basket. Suddenly there was a loud crash, as the cucumber bottle smashed to the ground. Gavin had reasoned that if he got rid of the container he could gain access to his cucumber without delay.

Small children like to learn new skills and this takes patience and time. It may not always be possible to let a child practise his newly acquired skill in buttoning a cardigan or tying laces when running late, but he usually gets enough opportunities to try out these simple tasks when his parents are less rushed. He wants to do things on his own, but on the other hand, he needs attentive, sensitive guidance from a parent who will take the time to encourage him in his efforts.

A child can develop best when he feels that his more baby-like dependent needs have been understood and treated with respect. Yet he also needs to feel that his parents have faith in his ability to grow, develop and learn new skills. If they continue to "baby" him, doing everything for him, he may sense this as confirmation that he isn't capable of doing anything by himself. On the other hand a child who has been pushed to do things for himself too early, finds it difficult to rely on others for help or guidance.

There are large variations in the speed and progress of language and physical development within the normal range, and children learn different skills at different times. Parents inevitably compare notes about their children's growing abilities and this can lead to a kind of competitiveness between them. They may worry if their child is not developing as fast as others but each child will progress at his own pace. There is only reason for concern if a child is seriously delayed in all his development and then professional advice should be sought.

## Part of the family

The immediate family forms the basis of the child's world and provides him with a "secure base" (a concept developed by the child psychiatrist John Bowlby, arising from his ideas about "attachment" as essential to human relationships) from which to venture out into the world. He observes and listens closely, copying actions, gestures and mannerisms. He relies on his parents' love and willingness to try and understand what he is trying to communicate through his behaviour, play and speech. Their love, protection and attention to his physical and emotional needs are the building blocks which enable him to develop empathy for others, to make meaningful relationships, and to learn from his experiences.

Around this time there may be major life issues to consider which affect the whole family. It is often a time when work demands are high, career changes or promotions may be considered, a new baby or house move could also be in the air. There may be grandparents, other family members and friends living nearby, to help share the load, but in these days of great mobility there is no guarantee that families will live nearby. Children may have to manage long-distance relationships with grandparents who live abroad, and they need their parents to help them with photos and reminders of family far away. We may mistakenly assume that children understand the concept of family members living a distance away but when asked where his granny lived (Jamaica), three-year-old Jason said, "She lives in the telephone!" Life with a three-year-old is full of contrasts and agendas to juggle which can make it exhausting as well as rewarding. Taking a short break to recharge batteries, even if it means just a quick walk to the shops, or an outing to the cinema, should be on any parent's priority list.

## Managing separation and transitions

One of the major tasks of small children and their parents is to manage the process of separation from each other, as children expand their horizons and move into social settings outside of the home. Preparing for and managing the settling-in period at nursery is a huge experience for parent and child, providing a model for future separations. Many parents send their children to nursery as early as possible because they believe it is "good" for them to get used to being with other children so as to settle easily into school.

This is not necessarily true – those children who have had a satisfying experience of one-to-one time with mother (or father) in their early babyhood often manage better when they enter group care because they have inside them a secure picture of a caring parent figure with whom they have had an exclusive relationship. This makes it easier at a later stage to share their parents with siblings, or the nursery teacher with a group of rival children, all longing to have teacher, like a mother, to themselves. Patterns of behaviour usually begin within the family, with the relationship a child has developed with his main carers. His attitude to and expectations of the outside world will depend to a large extent on his experiences of home life with the adults closest to him.

## What you will find in this book

In this book I shall try to bring to life the world of the three-year-old: his emotional ups and downs, his developing ability to play, learn and think, and his increasing physical and verbal skills. As we know, children are unique and develop along their own individual paths, but three-year-olds are also alike in many ways. The book includes examples of children from a range of social and ethnic backgrounds and their specific life experiences; I hope at least some of these examples will be familiar to you. I shall describe some of the ordinary trials, concerns and delights of having a three-year-old child, and will also suggest at what point mild difficulties or behavioural eccentricities could be worrying and require help outside the family. It is worth bearing in mind that even the most difficult and provocative behaviour in a three-year-old calms down in subsequent years and may contribute to the vitality of a child's developing personality. Life would be pretty dull if we all conformed to the same way of thinking and doing things!

# 1

# Understanding your Child

## Temperament and life experience

As parents well know, each of their children is unique, with their own character, likes and dislikes, fears and passions. What makes up this unique developing personality? How a three-year-old thinks, feels and behaves is in part connected to her relationship with her parents as a baby.

How she copes with new experiences like going to nursery, or a change of teacher, depends on how she was helped to deal with earlier frustrations, transitions and developments, for example, weaning or learning how to crawl. To some extent her parents' own experiences of being parented will also influence things. Sometimes parents will have had very different childhood experiences, perhaps even in different countries and cultures. Working to help a child develop confidence in her growing abilities, and to provide firm boundaries for her, is a challenge and a rewarding task.

But a baby is also born with her own innate temperament, and this, together with her early life experiences, will lead her to form her unique inner picture of the world. Her experience of early relationships will influence whether she sees the world as a mainly friendly, hopeful and understanding place, or as discouraging and hostile. What sort of welcome can she expect? How these relationships develop is also, in part, up to her. Is she an easily satisfied or demanding child? Is she slow to respond or does she gratify others with instant smiles?

By three, many of her patterns of relating and her expectations of others will have been established, but she will continue to develop new relationships and her picture of the world will keep on changing. The child has images or pictures inside her mind which accompany every action and thought. It is the content of these images that children often express in their behaviour, play and conversation. Close observation of and attentive listening to the detail of their play and actions can help us in our efforts to try and understand what is on a child's mind, what her interests and concerns are as she goes about her daily activities.

## The work of play

It is easy for us to underestimate the value and importance of play for children but in reality, play is a child's work, her way of developing her imagination, creativity and emotional life. We can see the absorbed concentration on a child's face as she plays with her train set, sets out a farm, acts out a story. Play takes many forms and has many functions for a child. Sometimes it is about sorting out the difference between fantasy and reality, trying out a range of roles and identities, working out ways of coping with intense feelings such as love, jealousy or anger. Children play out their hopes and fears often ascribing these feelings to their dolls, toy animals and other play things. Play is a child's way of working through her own life experiences: worries about separation, getting lost or being left behind, excited delight at learning new skills, fears of exclusion, sibling rivalry, all are among many of the themes that emerge in children's play at this age. A child may lay out farm scenes and leave a toy lamb bleating that it has "lost its mummy" then joyfully reunite them, or surround a sow with piglets all pushing in to make sure they have a teat to suckle. Hide-and-seek games have endless appeal, as they are a child's way of playing out worries about separation, and "losing" someone, then finding her again. Small children have a limited ability to bear the suspense of too long a wait in hiding and often make sure they are "found" before too long.

Since most of the time children have so little control over their lives (the comings and goings of those around them, the arrival of siblings, and so on), this is their opportunity to "take charge". They will excel at making tea, preparing dinner for or soothing a sick baby doll, pretend to go off to the shops or work leaving the teddy "children" at home.

## Fantasy worlds

Over the course of the fourth year the child's imaginary life becomes increasingly complex and she can spend long stretches of time wrapped up in make-believe games on her own or with a playmate. They may take on the role of a superhero from TV programmes like Batman or Shredder (Teenage Mutant Ninja Turtles), disappear into Teletubby Land talking in sing-song voices, or play at being princes, knights with swords, queens and fairies.

How delightful to have magical powers, strength and potency. With a wand food can magically appear, there is no need to rely on Mummy to provide it; injuries can be instantly healed, "baddies" can be killed off. Imagine how difficult it must feel for a small child to be constantly aware of all the things she cannot do by herself, all the skills she has yet to master, all the good things she is still totally dependent on her parents to deliver. She needs to have some escape into a make-believe world where she can take on the role of being in charge and triumphing over all danger. It can sometimes be difficult for small children to tell where fantasy ends and external reality begins and the imaginary play can be so involving that aspects of the game get mixed up with ordinary life. Children love their parents to join in their games as long as they do not become over-involved and controlling. They need adults to stand back enough to be able to stop a game if it becomes too frightening, and help the child return to outside reality.

Charlie and Tim were playing in the garden, running through piles of crunchy leaves. Charlie's six-year-old brother Pete whizzed past on his bike, hopped off and began a rough "leaf fight" with the younger boys, gradually burying them in leaves. Charlie looked a bit panicked as leaves piled on top of him, but he clambered out and he and Tim pretended to be on a boat. They made a mast out of the garden broom, with mother's help, while his brother cycled off. There was a bit of a squabble as to who would be captain, which mother helped to resolve. Soon the boys were rowing through a swirling "sea" of leaves. They couldn't get out of the boat because there were "loads of fierce sharks about". When mum called them in for tea Charlie began to look worried and called to mum to come and "rescue" them because "the sharks are after us!" The threat of sharks felt real to him and he couldn't be persuaded to step out of the boat without holding tightly onto his mother's hand.

Small children experience intense emotions such as anger, fear and hatred which can overwhelm them and quickly come spilling out. Charlie may have felt frightened and angry towards his brother for his rough treatment, perhaps he felt like attacking and biting him. These feelings were too much for him to manage and suddenly there seemed to be danger everywhere, particularly in the imaginary shark, which now seemed to contain Charlie's angry biting feelings – no wonder he felt afraid and anxious.

After tea Charlie said: "I want to ride like Pete on my bike." His mother suggested he had a go on his own. His tricycle was a bit big for him and he struggled to push it along the path. When he got it onto the grass it became even more difficult as his feet kept slipping off the pedals. Eventually he said grumpily that he wanted his mother to push him and she agreed. Mum took hold of the front of Charlie's tricycle and pulled him through the leaves, but Charlie screamed furiously, "Push from behind!" As she pushed the back of the trike, Charlie sailed along beaming, looking for all the world as if he was doing it all by himself, just like his big brother!

Perhaps at that moment, with his helping mother out of his sight, he could really believe he was riding on his own; that he was big brother, strong, powerful and beyond hurt or humiliation.

## Feeling small and managing feelings

As we could see with Charlie, parents sometimes have to put up with being treated like an accessory, an extension of the child, to enable him to feel competent and show off his prowess. It is important, of course, not always to do things for a child in this way, giving him the illusion that he possesses more skills than he actually has, because this may make it difficult for him to bear the ordinary sometimes painstakingly slow process of learning a new skill. A child who cannot tolerate feelings of frustration, who sees "not knowing" as a sign of weakness to be despised, may have difficulty learning new skills or listening to the teacher at school. In order to learn from others we have to be able to tolerate that "little child" feeling of not knowing.

## Potency: I can do anything

Three-year-olds revel in their rapidly developing skills, and at times feel enormously powerful. Anthony was taken to watch a fireworks display on Guy Fawkes Night. As the rockets flared up into the night sky, Anthony's hands moved up and down in rhythm, like a conductor, and he mouthed silently "I did it!" at each explosion. It was clear that he had become caught up in a fantasy where he was the powerful creator of these glittering rockets, gazed at and admired by hundreds of revellers.

Although excited by his powers, the child needs an adult to be keeping a watchful eye for the moment when everything becomes too much for him and he collapses into tears, until with help he can venture forth into the world again.

## Imaginary friends

Sometimes children develop an imaginary friend, like Binker, Christopher Robin's long-suffering companion in *Winnie-the-Pooh*, to help them manage feelings of exclusion or loneliness.

Pippa found it difficult to play on her own while her mother was feeding the baby. She disappeared, and returned some time later to say that she had had a lovely picnic with Susan. Her mother gathered that Susan was an imaginary friend and asked where she was now. Pippa said airily that she was away on holiday, becoming a little flustered when her mother persisted in asking where she had gone.

Imaginary figures or stuffed animals can be useful for a child to transfer some of her feelings onto, particularly those feelings she might like to keep a distance from: for example, if she is trying to be a big girl, it might be her "friend" who feels frightened of the dark, dogs or noisy dustbin vans.

## Telling the difference between fantasy and reality

Children of this age fluctuate in their ability to grasp reality and permanence, at times believing that anything and everything is possible. For example Josh told his mother, "When I am a girl I will have long hair!" Sometimes younger three-year-olds become determined to shape their world in exactly the way they want it, even if it doesn't quite fit in with reality. This may become more noticeable when a child is faced with a possibly worrying situation, or a change in routine.

Tessa had a slight fever and her grandmother was looking after her while her mother, a doctor, was at work. Tessa said, "Granny, my mummy's a doctor, she makes children better." Her granny agreed and said that her mummy was working and she, granny, was going to be looking after her. Tessa said: "Well, you're a doctor too!" Her granny said she wasn't. "Well," persisted Tessa, "you're a little bit a doctor." Her granny did not persist in denying it, but left it at that.

Tessa, who was missing her mummy, had to find a way of coping with a reality which was not what she wanted. Her way of managing was to transform the situation – Granny was the mummy doctor she needed near her while she felt unwell.

## Managing stressful times

One need only take a look around a nursery at the beginning of the new term to see how many children come dressed as fairies, gauze wings fluttering, wands waving, or wearing policemen's helmets or carrying an old briefcase of Daddy's and a toy mobile phone. A phone helps them feel in emotional contact with absent parents. These accessories and the way in which they allow children to imagine themselves as having special powers, can help children get through stressful times, when they might otherwise collapse into tears.

Suzie wore her Barbie Doll outfit to playgroup every day for the first month. When her teacher called her name, she said, "I am Barbie" and became upset if anyone called her Suzie. It seemed as if at that time she really did believe she was Barbie. The nursery workers were unsure how to approach this – did they agree to call her by that name, or force her to get in touch with reality? In the end, after discussion with her parents, they agreed to let Suzie play this game until the morning "circle time", after which she would take off her outfit and "become" Suzie again. This arrangement helped Suzie settle into nursery, and soon she no longer needed her Barbie persona.

## Questioning the magic

Children's powers of reason are developing and they may also start questioning the make-believe stories which until now have been taken for granted. They may wonder how the "tooth fairy" collects teeth or "Father Christmas" brings the presents and there may be a weaving together of practical concerns and make-believe.

Three-year-old Rose began asking her parents about Father Christmas, and how exactly he was going to get down the chimney. She wouldn't stop and her parents thought she seemed excited but also a little anxious about a strange man coming into their house in the middle of the night. So they told her that Father Christmas was just "pretend" and he wouldn't really be coming down the chimney. "But what will he do with all the presents?" was her reply. We can see how the worlds of reality and of make-believe collide for Rose, who cannot instantly give up the clear picture she has in her mind of Father Christmas carrying a sack of gifts down the chimney.

## The development of conscience and empathy

A small child has a powerful imagination which can produce extreme versions of familiar figures, either more perfect or more threatening than the "real" people they are meant to represent. These figures (ideal and fairy god-mother-like or frightening and witch-like) are created in infancy when a baby experiences extreme states of feeling blissfully satisfied or intensely uncom-fortable. They certainly do not resemble the "real" parents of everyday life. Parents overhearing their children play out an imaginary family scene may be shocked to find themselves portrayed in a cruel light, responding to bad behaviour with harsh threats or even a beating. Are they *really* as strict as their children portray them in their games?

These fierce figures of the imagination are created partly from a child's own hostile feelings and partly from a sense that aggressive thoughts or acts must be punished. This is how a "guilty conscience" develops. When a child refuses to own up to some wrongdoing or blames someone else, we cannot assume that she has no conscience, but rather that her conscience is too severe and the imagined punishments too frightening to contemplate. It may be safer to get rid of all feelings of responsibility and blame someone else.

However, a child's conscience tells her she *should* be punished for her wrongdoing, and her inner voice is far less forgiving than her real parents would be. A child will sometimes go on and on deliberately provoking a parent, goading him on as if she wants to be smacked. She occasionally succeeds in provoking a harsh punishment as parents reach the end of their tether – punishment is felt to be preferable to feelings of guilt and upset about the hurt or damage she has caused. Sometimes children can be seen hitting themselves or banging their heads as a form of self-punishment or they may become temporarily more accident-prone, falling and hurting themselves soon after having caused hurt or damage to others.

Children also have a picture of an ideal, admirable parent in mind, whom they strive to emulate and be worthy of. Children love to please their parents and long for approval. Letting a child know what pleases or displeases is often the most effective form of discipline.

If a child has the experience of parents who offer understanding and firmness rather than punishment, she learns to empathize with others, as they have done with her. She begins to feel regret for her angry behaviour and may wish to make things better. Fixing things and identifying with adults in helpful roles, such as police officers or nurses, are an important form of children's play.

## Language and conversation

The child's attempts to imitate and pronounce words continue to delight those around her, as she may still name a butterfly a "flutter by" or humorously cling onto names for siblings first coined before she could fully pronounce them. When she was a baby Molly had thought ice cream was called "some", since her parents always asked her if she wanted "some" when she passed an ice-cream stall. This went down as part of the family myth, and formed a humorous bond between them.

Sometimes children's precocious delight in language and their increased confidence in expressing themselves can lead to embarrassment for parents, as their children are quite uninhibited about their observations. Reena was travelling on the bus with her mother, who noticed she was staring at the old lady across the aisle. Then at the top of her voice Reena pointed to the lady saying, "Mum she's got a big spot [wart] on her nose, just like the witch in my book *Each Peach Pear Plum*...and she's got the same black stockings and...". At this point her mother spoke to her quietly and suggested that she talk in a softer voice because she may be disturbing the other passengers. Although she felt embarrassed she did not scold Reena, but smiled apologetically to the woman and left it at that.

Three-year-olds like to invent words for themselves, talking about "shaky" (long) hair. They use their powers of reason and come up with words that make logical sense, such as "goodest", "beautifulest". It is important that children feel free to try out new words without being shy or self-conscious. Children who may have been corrected too harshly, or those who cannot bear to make mistakes, may refuse to speak until they are sure they will get things right. They need to have other children and adults around who can talk to them and spend time answering their questions.

Language is also a way for children to make sense of the world around them, as well as their own experiences and emotions. When a child is able to put her ideas and feelings into words and to "speak her mind", she has made a huge developmental leap. Her ability to think about and make sense of her experiences is revealed in her capacity to express them verbally.

If she is very upset or excited a child's feelings might overwhelm her and erupt in running about, hitting out or shouting. But at calmer times, with adult help, children may be able to put their feelings into words.

Lunchtime at the nursery had been difficult for Asaf; his key worker was off sick and a child had grabbed a carrot stick off his plate, unseen by the adults. The stand-in worker didn't know that Asaf hated different foods touching each other, and had dolloped yoghurt onto his tinned pears. Asaf got down from the table, wandered off and tipped a large bowl of salad onto the unsuspecting head of another child. Staff reacted with understandable anger, and Asaf refused to say he was sorry or to help tidy up despite threats and ultimatums. Asef left the mess and lay down on the floor. Eventually, once he had comforted and cleaned up the other child, the worker went over to talk to him:

Worker: Are you upset?

Asaf:     Speak to me.

Worker: Why did you throw the salad? Were you angry?

Asaf:     You made me upset just an hour ago.

Worker: What did I do?

Asaf:     You gave me white poo.

Worker: You didn't want yoghurt, yes?

Asaf:     I just wanted pears.

Worker: Are you still angry with me?

Asaf:     I wanted you to cuddle me. (*The worker moved towards him.*)

Asaf:     Not now, wanted you to do it and you didn't.

Asaf could not manage his feelings of shock and anger, passing them on to another child along with the salad. He had felt misunderstood and ignored, and conveyed this feeling by ignoring all requests to help tidy up. However, when the worker showed an interest in understanding the meaning of his behaviour, Asaf was able to verbalize his feelings and to share them.

Repeated experiences of feeling understood will gradually enable Asaf to put his feelings into words and his unprovoked attacks on other children are likely to diminish.

## Curiosity and questions

Most small children will be bursting with curiosity, keen to explore space, size and distances. They will want to know about different materials and about sounds and what produces them. They will be interested in how things work, including the human body, keen to know what goes on inside – whether it is a car, a machine, or a person. Their antennae will be out to absorb snippets of adult conversation, observing interactions going on around them and asking questions.

A child's interest in exploring and trying to make sense of her world depends to some extent on her temperament, but also on her having had parents who have shown an interest in her and her developing mind. If she has had parents who have done their best to make sense of her behaviour and communications in her early years, she will have absorbed into herself a similar enthusiasm for understanding and learning and in this way she will develop a healthy curiosity about the world. Her questions may be direct and awkward, and she may well ask about the conception and birth of children, about her parents' sexual relationship to each other and about death, at inconvenient times. She may ask unanswerable metaphysical questions like "Where was I before I was born?" Parents may not be able to answer these questions fully or immediately, but it is important for children to feel that their questions have been taken seriously and that an attempt has been made to respond to their interest.

Sometimes the endless questions and "why's?" seem to be a small child's means of staying in the conversation, keeping the adult's attention, and keeping rival siblings at bay. Children may ask questions as a way of "holding onto" adults, particularly if they are feeling a little insecure. Vicky's godmother decided to visit some friends for tea before taking Vicky home after a day out together. When told about this change of plan Vicky asked, "Why?" Further explanations simply led to more and more questions. Eventually Vicky's godmother realized that giving rational answers was not helping and instead she reassured Vicky that her mother knew about the changed arrangement and would be at home for her when she returned. Vicky relaxed – she hadn't been interested in the explanations but in holding onto her godmother's attention until her worries about seeing her mother had been understood.

# 2

# Family Life

## Developing family relationships

The parents, immediate family and home are the centre of the three-year-old's world. He may be venturing out to nursery or interacting occasionally with relative strangers but his strongest emotional ties will be to his parents. They already have a long history together and some major milestones have been achieved such as walking and development of speech. Early losses, such as being weaned from the breast or bottle or separating from mother if she has returned to work, have been negotiated, easily for some, less easily for others.

By three, the child's feelings for mother and father will have undergone many changes and fluctuations, with sometimes father, sometimes mother in favour. At times the couple together will be lovingly regarded, at other times jealously hated. If there is a sibling the two children may occasionally join together to "gang up" on the parents. If mother and father are living together, and even when they are not, the child will have an inkling at some level, that his parents have a separate and private relationship between them, of which he is not a part. A three-year-old is very aware of his parents' relationship as a *couple*. He can feel intensely jealous of this relationship and become aware that he is excluded from this area. If parents sit together for a cuddle on the sofa, he is likely to squeeze in between them.

He may become angrily frustrated by his own small child's limitations, longing to have the strength and power of Daddy or Mummy's rich supplies of food, love and beauty. It is perfectly natural for a little girl of this age (or younger) to fantasize about getting Mummy out of the way and having Daddy all to herself, or for a boy to passionately embrace his Mummy, while glaring at his Daddy as if telling him to "Keep off, she's mine!"

## The Oedipus complex

The term Oedipus complex was coined by Sigmund Freud, who drew our attention to the now commonly recognized pattern of feelings that gets stirred up between young children and the parent of the opposite sex. He based his ideas on the ancient Greek myth which describes how Oedipus unknowingly killed his father and married his mother. This is not meant to be taken literally, but as shorthand to describe the jealous longings that a child of one sex has for a parent of the opposite sex. This possessive desire makes the child wish he could get rid of (or 'kill off') the rival for his adored parent's affections and these are known as Oedipal feelings. These may not always be conscious thoughts but imaginary pictures that accompany the child's possessive behaviour towards one parent and attempts to exclude the other.

Most parents have heard their child declare his love for them saying, "When I'm older I'm going to marry you!" to one parent, ignoring the fact that the parent in question is already married. This can feel hurtful to the excluded parent, who might respond angrily. It can be helpful to consider that a small child often gets others to understand how *he* is feeling by behaving in ways that will stir up these same feelings in *them*. So, in this case, the child's hurt feelings about being the one left out of the parent couple are passed on to the "left-out" parent, who gets first-hand experience of what this feels like. His actions seem to be saying, "Let him/her see what it feels like to be excluded."

Nico and his parents always went on a Sunday family outing into the countryside, and it was the highlight of their week. As the weather grew warmer they sometimes stopped to swim in a river. On one occasion his mother stripped down to her bra and pants for a quick dip. As she came out dripping Nico ran up to her, touched her bra and said wistfully, "Oh I do love breast-y – she is so beautiful!" Mother replied, "And you are my beautiful little boy!" As they were setting off home Nico demanded to sit in the front seat next to his mother, ordering his father to "sit in the back where the children go!" His parents were puzzled as he hadn't shown an interest in sitting in the front before, and they stood firm, insisting that sitting strapped into his car seat was the safest place for Nico.

## Mother's beauty and erotic feelings

We can see how Nico's passions are quickly stirred up by seeing his mother's partially exposed body. It seems to have evoked early memories of his experience at the breast as a baby, of the beauty of his mother as he gazed into her eyes (and she into his), stroked her breast and felt the warm milk fill him up. These early memories of mother and baby closeness remain inside a child's mind and help cushion him against frustrating or difficult times. Such early sensual feelings, together with the upsurge of intense Oedipal feelings, combined to arouse Nico's passion for his mother. This led him to attempt to displace his father, by insisting on the front seat next to mother in the car.

## Jealousy and its link to sleep difficulties

When these jealous and passionate feelings are at their height in small children, they may result in sleep difficulties. Parents often complain that their child has a knack of "knowing" just when they might be enjoying a moment of intimacy, and choose that moment to call for a bottle or appear in the doorway. Children who wake many times through the night, for no obvious reason, may well be waking to keep a check on their parents' activities, particularly if there is talk of another baby in the air.

Three-year-old Penny had started waking three or four times during the night, when she was usually a sound sleeper, and she always called for Daddy. At this time her favourite activity was dressing up in mother's hats and shoes, with the occasional dab of make-up. Her mother noticed that she tended to deck herself out in this way towards the end of the day when father was due back home. She would rush to the door before mother or one-year-old Don could reach it, grab Daddy's hand and show him her latest drawing (one of the drawings showed Mummy very small, looking like a little girl, and Penny and Daddy the same size, holding hands).

One day Penny needed a wee just around the time her father was due home, and she struggled so long with her dungaree clasps that she wet herself. When father arrived home he was met with a distraught Penny, who cried and wouldn't look at him while mother cleaned her up.

Another evening Penny showed her parents her latest drawing, a page full of shapes, triangles, circles, squares. She told them that her favourite shape was a circle and her worst was a triangle. As bedtime drew near she asked mother if she could wear her wedding ring, and mother let her try it on. Penny gave her a ring she had found in a lucky dip in compensation. Penny went and lay spread-eagled across her father's lap, and said: "I am married to Daddy now, Mummy is Don's and Daddy is mine!"

We can see why a circle would appeal to her with its smooth surface and sense of continuity and sameness, while a triangle, with its three corners, seems to be shouting out, "Three's a crowd!" Her parents began to put two and two together, and to wonder whether Penny's night waking might have something to do with this phase she was going through. The fact that they had discussed this issue together, and had some ideas about the underlying reason for this new behaviour, helped them to be more understanding. While they continued to show affection towards each other, they were careful not to provoke her jealousy, continued to be firm about her remaining in her own bed at night and stuck to alternating rotas for getting up to be with her. Over time her sleeping pattern gradually improved.

## Sleeping alone

Most young children think that their parents' bed is the best and most comfortable bed in the whole world, and often long to sleep enfolded in its special covers. The parents' bed holds some exciting mystery of which a child is aware. Three-year-old Tessa flopped on her parents' bed saying, "This is a big bed." Her mum replied that it had to fit two people in, Mummy and Daddy. Tessa said, "But I want a big bed like that too." Her mum explained that when she was grown-up she would get married and share a big bed with her husband. Tessa replied, "Yes, with Tom!" (her father).

By calling her father "Tom" instead of "Daddy" Tessa seems to be blurring the generational boundaries between parent and child, perhaps hoping this will give her a better chance in the wooing game.

Children often complain about the injustice of having to sleep in a small bed alone while their parents have each other for company. After all, as Tessa continued, "One little girl has to sleep on her own, and two *grown-ups* have each other!"

Young children often complain loudly about things not being fair, and are very sensitive to issues around fairness, distribution of food, gifts or attention. This may stem from the fact that, despite their growing competence and skills, they are mainly dependent on caring adults to support and nurture them. The exclusive relationship parents have with each other, of which the child cannot be a part, may be the source of this feeling of unfairness.

## Managing these feelings in small children

It is useful to be aware of how stimulating and possibly troubling it can be for a child to be too exposed to his parents' sexual life. It is an area which a child needs to know exists, as proof of his parents' love of each other, but does not need to see or hear.

Parents find themselves being more cautious about bathing together with a three-year-old child, or walking around in the nude. This does not imply that a prissy self-conscious attitude needs to be cultivated around nudity or bodily functions, but parents often become extra aware of how arousing things can be for a child who might not be able to manage the feelings that are stirred up. When one parent is away it is so tempting to let a child sleep "on Daddy's side". This can stimulate the child's fantasy that he really has got rid of Daddy (although in reality he may know perfectly well that he is away working) and now has Mummy all to himself. This can apply to parents of the same sex as the child, and to lone parents as well. It may feel comforting for a lone parent and child to share a bed, but it can create a sense of confusion in a three-year-old who, in his fantasy life, may feel his rightful place is in bed next to his mother.

Whether a partner is physically present or not, it is important for the child to have an idea in his mind of a parent couple, and to feel that there is the possibility of a partner for his lone mother. He needs to know that his place is not in the parental bedroom, but in his own room. If a child has been sharing a bed with his lone parent, and a partner then comes on the scene, or father stays over occasionally, the child may react badly, feeling that he has been pushed out of his proper place.

## Parents: some time together

All parents need a break from their children in order to renew their energy, refresh themselves and nurture their couple relationship. At the least they will be trying to get to the bottom of sleep difficulties if they are still having interrupted nights. It is important for the well-being of parents and child to make sure that they have some protected space for relaxation.

By the time a child is three his parents will have left him with a family member, friend or childminder, for a few hours a week, if not longer. There may be a window of opportunity for parents to take a short break away on their own. This would depend on there being reliable carers willing to take on his care for a weekend (or even just overnight) and would need careful preparation. It may be possible for a carer to move into the family home, so that the child can remain in his familiar environment and follow his normal routine. A child's grasp of time at that age is not well established and he may need the help of a simple calendar, with clear markings to show which days parents will be away and when they will be returning. The child's *sense* of how long his parents have been absent is what really counts and if they are away more than a couple of days it could begin to feel as if they'll be away forever. Short breaks are likely to be more manageable for a small child than longer periods of a week or more away.

## Reunion after separation

Their child might have coped well while they were away, but on their return he may show the strain he has been under by regressing a little, or being less exuberant than usual. He might turn away, give them "the cold shoulder" when they greet him to show his annoyance at having been left. It is important that parents continue to be friendly and welcoming to the child despite his frosty response, as in this way things should soon thaw between them and relationships continue as before.

If a parent has been away (at work for example) a three-year-old may not rush to greet him. The parent may have to go looking for a child who may have hidden himself away. He wants Daddy to search for him so that Daddy can know what it feels like to miss someone and to have to wait until he reappears. If the parent can be humorous about it, and can make it into a game of hide and seek, then the trust between parent and child can be re-established.

Salima and her mum had baked a chocolate cake for tea, and when her dad came home from work the first thing Salima said was, "We baked a *delicious* cake and there's *none* left for you!" In fact, the cake was virtually untouched, but Salima had made her point. She had been deprived of her father all day and it was only fair that he should feel deprived of something equally special. Father took this in his stride and after supper sat her on his lap to read her favourite storybook.

## Identification with parents and developing an identity

Although a child has his own temperament and personality, much of what he becomes is powerfully influenced by his parents. Jake's mother described how he was mesmerized by the window cleaner, chatted to the workmen mending the dishwasher, following them around the house and insisting on having his lunch with them. He seemed to connect them with his Daddy, and may have been imagining what it might feel like to be him. But Jake was also observing his mother with great interest.

Jake's mother was baking a blackberry pie and had set Jake up with a toy oven and food. Jake picked up a tea towel from the table and used it to pick up his toy pie tin carefully, as he had seen his mother do. Holding the edge of the pie tin he walked over to his toy oven, opened the door, and carefully put the pie in, turning on the timer, and humming to himself, "The pie's in now, shouldn't be too long, pie, pie, pie." He returned to the table, and began tidying away the mixing bowls, softly singing his "pie song". He set the table with toy plates and declared his pie ready. He dragged the knife around the edge of the pie tin to ensure that the pie didn't stick to the sides and lifted it up. There was a sense of real joy in him as he slipped the pie out of the tin, as if he had taken inside himself a "singing, pie-making Mummy".

Jake must have observed the details of this activity many times; he seems to have absorbed not just his mother's baking style but also her quiet concentration on the task, her sense of joy at creating something good. In order to be able to give such loving attention to his task, Jake would need to have experienced the same kind of caring attentiveness by parents or others close to him over a long period of time. This way he can identify with these qualities of joyful concentration and eventually, they will become a part of his developing personality. The knowledge that he can have this kind of happy experience, and can occupy himself creatively, will stand him in good stead and may give him an optimistic outlook on life. At the least, he will have something good inside to fall back on when things go wrong, and he is faced with ordinary frustrations or upsets.

The child needs a parent figure from whom to learn and who can be admired. It is not possible to always behave in admirable ways but usually he gains enough good experiences to use as a role model. A little boy who feels that Daddy is his rival for Mummy can become quite triumphant when Daddy is incompetent or makes mistakes. Children's stories sometimes amplify this notion showing parents (or one parent) as incompetent (while the other can be depicted as rather smug) or unreliable. These books can be humorous and clearly appeal to the aspect of children that enjoys seeing these all-powerful parents as the foolish figures. *The Bike Lesson* by Stan and Jan Berenstain depicts this kind of situation, where father bear sets out to teach his son how to ride a bike, but gets everything wrong – it is a lesson in how *not* to ride a bike.

## Parents getting on together

Getting on well together when looking after one or more children under five can be a strain for both partners. Both may be trying to work, exist on less than the optimal amount of sleep and may struggle to find time and space to be together in a relaxed way. The small child feels most safe when he senses that his parents are coexisting more or less harmoniously, with the usual ups and downs. While feeling jealous of his parents' affection for each other, he becomes anxious if he sees them constantly at each other's throats. It can make him feel unsafe and unheld. Because of his mixed feelings towards his parents as a loving couple a child will often feel responsible for bad "vibes" between parents, as if his wishes to separate them may actually have come true.

Three-year-old Patrick was sitting in the kitchen when his mum came in, handed him his coat and irritably told him to "Go and tell your father that I've found your coat"...then, under her breath, she said: "'cos I'm not talking to him". Father came in and asked where the coat had been found and mother didn't answer him. Patrick went out and suddenly called his mother saying he was frightened of the stairs. She came up the stairs with him and he wanted to play doctors with her, insisting that she was "hurt". He made his mother sit on his beanbag and pull up the leg of her jeans. He treated her "pretend" cut knee by dabbing pretend cotton wool on and giving her a "dangerous" injection.

Patrick probably heard his mother's comments about his father and picked up the tense "dangerous" atmosphere between his parents. He might have felt that these big and powerful people, who seemed like enemies that day, could do terrible things to each other, and where would that leave him? This may be why he became suddenly fearful. He tried to find a visible reason for mother's upset feelings, inventing a cut knee, and putting himself in a role where he could be the doctor and sort everything out.

## Parenting roles

Although each parent will bring his or her own style and personality to parenting, a child needs to feel that each parent individually is able to be a tender, comforting figure, as well as firm and boundary- setting. Sometimes a division occurs where one parent takes on the firm, limit-setting role, while the other takes on the role of comforting and nurturing the child. This can cause confusion as the child is faced with an extreme division of roles. It can feel safer for a child if both parents are able to take on both roles, because it enables each parent to provide both kinds of care for the child without relying on the other to be present.

Some couples work hard to ensure that their child has a picture of each parent being able to provide both firmness and kindness together, but for other couples this is more difficult. Similarly, some lone parents are able to combine both these roles within themselves, whereas other lone parents find it extremely difficult to hold onto the firm "father" type of role as well as the nurturing "mother" type of role.

## Driving a wedge between parents

Children can be very clever at playing one parent off against the other, which tends to cause resentment and rows between the adults, particularly if one parent is perceived to be more indulgent and "spoiling" and the other more strict. If a parent feels valued and appreciated by her partner it may be easier to put up with what might feel like quite painful rejection at times. A child may go through a period of wanting only one parent to put him to bed and the "chosen" parent might enjoy being the preferred one, secretly feeling triumphant over his partner. We all have infantile feelings at times, and can feel competitive for our child's affection. The less favoured parent may have to put up with these feelings for a while, but not necessarily give in to the child's demands. The child feels relieved to have proof that in the end his parents have control over the situation, and not himself.

A child learns about respecting other's feelings if he has a model of parents who respect each other and him, demonstrating a thoughtful considerate way of relating to others. If one parent is always being "put down" or undermined by another, it can affect the child's identification with that parent. He may not want to be on the "losing side" and may feel obliged to join in with the criticism or mockery.

## Differences of opinion about discipline

Sometimes there are extreme differences of opinion about discipline within families. For example, one parent believes in strict discipline and is perceived as the punishing "baddie" while the other parent is more indulgent and is seen as a "pushover" who "spoils" the child. When we add grandparents who may also have conflicting views about childcare, things can get difficult. These different approaches can create confusion and worry in small children, who may show signs of distress and anxiety as they try to make sense of the bewildering mixed messages they receive from the adults caring for them.

Three-year-old Andrew was being cared for in shifts during the week by his parents and both sets of grandparents, all of whom had extremely different approaches to disciplining him. He began to develop signs of distress, head-banging and having unmanageable tantrums.

Father was very strict and his expectations of Andrew were high, considering his age. Father needed only to lift up his finger or raise his voice, and Andrew would look frightened and instantly stop what he was doing. By contrast, mother hated to stop him doing anything, allowing him to empty out the contents of her handbag on to the floor of the living room, or raid the fridge, leaving a trail of mess behind him. She treated him like a much younger child and every time he cried she gave him a piece of furry cloth to hold which she took everywhere they went. Father insisted on strict order and routine, and punished Andrew if he wouldn't eat or go to bed. Mother didn't believe in set mealtimes or bedtimes. She felt he would "have routines for the rest of his life and he's only a baby". Andrew went to sleep when he "felt like it", sometimes falling asleep in the living room and being carried to bed. Andrew felt that he could run riot over his mother, had total access to her with no holds barred, and at the same time he felt frightened of and distant from his father. He could not relax and concentrate on playing if he kept needing to adjust to different expectations of him each time his carer changed.

We can imagine how these extreme differences in approach to his childcare might have contributed to Andrew's confusion and worry, resulting in his destructive behaviour.

## Putting aside rivalry and working together as parents

Sally and John were on holiday in Greece with three-year-old Martin and had hired a car for a couple of days to tour around the island. They came to a beautiful safe-looking sandy beach and hopped out for a swim. Martin was impatient to go and paddle in the shallow water while his parents were still changing. His mum told him to wait as they didn't know this beach, while his dad disagreed and said mum should stop being such a "worry-pot!" While they were bickering, Martin ran into the sea. Suddenly they heard him scream and rushed to him. He had run straight into a rocky patch that was covered with sea urchins and had been stung. They drove with a screaming Martin to the nearest town where they found a doctor who could speak a little English.

He would have to perform a small procedure to remove the spines from his heel.

Sally and John were tense and anxious, but now was not the time for recriminations and "I told you so"s. Martin cried for his Daddy to hold him, not Mummy, and she had to swallow her more child-like feelings about how unfair it was that Martin should want *Daddy* when, after all, *she* had been the one who had wanted to check out the beach first. While the doctor gave Martin an injection, John held Martin's hand and comforted him. They had brought Martin's favourite Buzz Lightyear toy in with them, and Sally stood with Buzz at the bottom of the bed telling Buzz all about what was happening to his foot, with Buzz making amusing and comforting replies. Martin was upset but coped well with his ordeal. He had been contained by parents who had managed to work together, "holding" him from the head down to the feet with their comforting words.

## Single parents

Most single parents are mothers living alone with their children, some out of choice, others because of relationship breakdown with the father. For some children father has never been around, for others he remains an important figure in their lives. The quality and frequency of contact children have with their fathers varies enormously depending on whether the parents have remained on good enough terms to negotiate regular consistent contact. In families where children have been living in a chronically tense or violent atmosphere, separation could come as a relief but contact arrangements become a new battleground.

By the age of three children will have noticed that some of their friends have fathers living at home and are bound to ask about their own absent fathers. It can be difficult for single mothers to give helpful information to their children without revealing their own angry or bitter feelings about their ex-partners where the separation has been acrimonious or violent. The child may pick up this attitude towards his father which could make him mistrustful or fearful of men in general. The child may imagine he was responsible for the break-up: perhaps if he had been better behaved or more charming his father might not have left the family. This can have an effect on a child's self-esteem. Parents can help by being honest about the difficulties while at the same time assuring a child that he has had no part to play in the separation. Sometimes small children become restless and have difficulty concentrating in nursery because they may be preoccupied with thoughts of an absent parent, particularly when contact is inconsistent and unreliable. They may become anxious, unsure whether and when father (or mother) will turn up for a visit, and the main carer is often left picking up the pieces if a child is let down.

Gabby was getting into difficulties at nursery, disrupting "circle time" (the quiet period when children listen to a story or have a group discussion with the teacher) with her restless activity and lack of concentration. On days when her father was due to collect her from nursery, Gabby found it difficult to settle down and play, jumping up to look out of the window, checking for her father's car. The key worker at nursery noticed that on these days Gabby spent a long time gluing at the craft table, sticking pieces of paper together and making sure they couldn't be pulled apart. On one of these days Gabby wouldn't let her key worker leave the craft table, and tried to sellotape the worker to his chair. In their staff meeting the worker discussed his observations with his colleagues, who wondered whether Gabby's interest in glue and her determination to stick the worker to his chair might be connected to her worry about father's unreliability, perhaps a wish to "stick" him close to her, to ensure he was there when he promised. Perhaps Gabby did not know how to express these feelings verbally, so she enacted with the nursery worker her wish to keep important people close to her. The staff group agreed that Gabby's feelings of uncertainty could be interfering with her ability to concentrate in circle time. It was a difficult situation for mother, who felt that if she "nagged" at father too much he might drop the contact altogether. However, at a meeting with the parents, the nursery staff highlighted Gabby's anxiety about whether and when she would be collected, and following on from this, father made greater efforts to ensure that he was on time or contacted the school if he was delayed. Over time Gabby became calmer and more able to concentrate in a relaxed way on her nursery activities.

# 3

# A New Baby in the Family

## Changes for everyone

### Making the decision

Making a decision about whether and when to try to conceive another baby may not always be straightforward. Parents struggling with a difficult three-year-old, who is going through a tyrannical, tantrum-filled phase, often say, "We wouldn't dream of another, she's enough for anybody!"…"We wouldn't do it to her, she's jealous enough as it is, a baby would only make things worse." Conversely they may talk about having another baby, "for *her* sake, so she won't be an only child". Making a decision to go ahead or not, based on the behaviour and needs of the existing child, can place quite a burden on her either way.

In truth small children are likely to have mixed feelings about a new baby that they may not be consciously aware of or be able to verbalize. Even if there is no baby yet the child may well have babies in mind – she may see her friends' mothers produce them, and wonder what is happening at home. At times she may attempt to keep her parents apart by provocative behaviour or by setting one parent up against the other, so that they end up arguing and not in the mood for making love. But she may also worry if she feels she is responsible for preventing them from having another baby. Her ability to differentiate fantasy from reality is increasing, but at times of stress she may become confused about just how powerful she is. If parents make an independent decision to have another baby, she may feel relieved because the arrival of a healthy baby confirms to her that her powers are limited, that she is, after all, still a little child, who needs to leave important decisions to the grown-ups. She has thus been helped to separate out fantasy from reality. Conversely, if a baby is tragically stillborn, born damaged or ill, the older child may feel that her fantasies of, for example, hurting or getting rid of the baby, are confirmed, and the belief that she has such power to destroy can make her feel frightened. If her parents recognize how guilty and anxious she feels about the power of her own wishes, she may feel reassured by their understanding and comfort.

## Termination

Sometimes parents decide to terminate a pregnancy for a variety of reasons. It is unlikely that they will tell the child directly about this, but she may well pick up in the atmosphere and through conversation, that something has happened to his mum that connects to the loss of a baby.

There are times when parents decide that they need some professional advice when they feel concerned about sudden or unusual behaviour. Many child guidance clinics have special services for families with children under five where a brief consultation and a couple of meetings together might be enough to get the family back on track.

Mrs Neville brought her child Darren to the Under Fives Service because he had suddenly started stuttering and stumbling over his words. When I met them together, mother seemed tired and depressed. Darren began playing with the toys, but couldn't settle for long. He kept running up to his mother, tugging at her sleeve, saying urgently, "You, you, you…must, must, I…I…I…", stumbling over his words as he struggled to get them out. He seemed to be trying to get her to come over and see what he was playing but she wasn't in the mood to be interested. I noticed that Darren didn't stutter when he was playing with the toy animals but only when he was trying to get his mother's attention. I asked mother whether there was anything in particular which might have caused her to be so otherwise preoccupied, because it seemed as if Darren wasn't used to having to struggle quite so much to get her attention and interest. I had begun to think that Darren's newly acquired stutter might be his way of forcing her to stop and listen as he spluttered out his words. It was his way of pulling her out of her depressed mood and holding onto her attention.

Mrs Neville then told me that she had been pregnant and that she and her husband had decided on a termination, as they did not feel they could cope with a fourth child, financially or emotionally. While we were discussing this

Darren took out a "mummy gorilla" and made the gorilla fiercely kick a baby chimpanzee right off the play table. We talked about this and I suggested to Mrs Neville that Darren had possibly picked up some idea about getting rid of babies (never far from small children's minds anyway), as his play with the baby chimpanzee had shown us. Perhaps if this is what parents do to unwanted children, he might fear he would be the next to be kicked out. This could be the cause of his stammer, his way of clinging tightly to her by taking so long to get out his words. Mrs Neville agreed that this made some sense, adding that she had noticed Darren had been more clingy to her lately, not letting her even have a shower in peace. After a few more meetings, where Darren played out several similar scenes with the animals and we talked together, his stutter disappeared.

## News of the pregnancy

A new baby in the family heightens many of the conflicts that all three-year-olds have, feeling like a small dependent baby at times, and at others feeling quite grown-up. Parents are often unsure when to tell a child about the new baby. If they leave it too late the child will hear from someone else, but knowing too early leads to a long wait. If the child has wished for a baby of a particular gender, the suspense can be difficult to manage unless parents decide to find out the sex of their baby beforehand. Either way a small child's curiosity and imagination will be stimulated by this momentous news.

Three-year-old Samantha's parents were rather surprised when, in response to the news of her mother's pregnancy, and their brief explanation of how babies were made, she exclaimed, "Well, why didn't you call me to come and watch!" She kept a close eye on them for a few weeks, was reluctant to go to bed at her usual bedtime and regularly crept downstairs at some point in the evening saying she couldn't sleep. Eventually her parents realized that she was quite worried and curious about what her parents were getting up to in her absence. They talked to her about how she seemed to be coming to check on them at night and allowed her to sit up with them for a few minutes.

On one of these occasions Samantha built a fence enclosure and put a "mummy" horse inside, carefully placing a "baby horse" close to the mummy. She built a second enclosure behind the sofa where her parents sat, and filled it with "millions of babies" (a selection of baby animals from her toy box). Her parents watched her play with interest, commenting to each other on how Samantha had hidden all the other baby animals from view except the one mummy horse and her foal. Perhaps she was worried that they were going to fill up the house with so many babies that there wouldn't be enough attention left over for her. Of course, if parents discover they will be having twins or triplets, this can confirm the child's fantasies of being overrun by babies.

Children of this age can be very tuned in to adults' conversations, and absorb much more than some people believe. Adults often converse and discuss quite intimate or inappropriate issues in the presence of children, assuming that they "won't understand" or are busy playing so they won't hear. This is not true. Sometimes children pick up fragments of a discussion or bits of information which they cannot make sense of. They can become confused and anxious about such troubling half-truths or distortions of reality.

Toby's single mother had recently conceived a baby by a fairly new boyfriend Chris. Toby overheard mother talking to her friend about how the pregnancy was "an accident" and "a disaster". When Chris arrived to take his mother out that evening Toby, who was used to his babysitter and usually enjoyed his time with her, became hysterical and clung onto his mother. Although she hadn't told Toby about the pregnancy yet, mother eventually understood that Toby was fearful that his mum would have 'an accident' while out with Chris.

## How are babies made?

Children have all sorts of fantasies about how a baby is made, and these are usually linked to their ideas about their own bodily functions. At this age children are very interested in what they do with their mouths – bite, chew, eat, swallow, talk, shout – as well as in their waste products, urine and faeces. It stands to reason that they will assume that similar methods are used for creating a baby, especially since in general adults talk about "Mummy having a baby in her *tummy*". Sylvie developed hiccoughs during lunchtime at nursery and told her classmates that her mummy got a baby by swallowing lots of air, "Then a baby burped out!"

Pete, who had been told that "the sperm meets egg" and "the baby comes out of a special passageway", amended this information to fit in with his theory based upon eating and excreting. "The sperm meets the egg in the mother's stomach" having found its way through her mouth in some mysterious fashion. The "special passageway" wasn't so special after all, it was either the one where the wee comes out or where the poo comes out. Young children do not have the capacity to conceptualize the sexual act and their fantasies can sometimes surprise parents, who think they have made the facts very clear.

## Brothers and sisters: friendship and jealousy

### Younger siblings

For a three-year-old the birth of a new baby can be a tremendous shock, but with careful handling the older child can be helped to recover and to enjoy the endless admiration that a baby will shower on her. Within any single day feelings will shift and change and parents have the task of juggling the needs of two small children, and attempting to attend to them all. Moments of joy and moments of jealousy or anger are all part of a day in the life of a young family.

Three-year-old Josie was playing outside when she spotted ten-month-old Sarah inside with her nose pressed up against the sliding door to the garden, watching her game. Grinning with delight she jumped up and began to play a "squashing noses against the glass" game with Sarah, until it was time for Sarah's feed.

Josie wandered in just as mother was saying to Sarah, "Let's look at your nursery rhyme book." Josie immediately produced a large farm floor puzzle saying, "I want to play the puzzle." "Let's find the horse for Sarah", mum suggested, and together they picked up the puzzle piece and put it in front of her. Josie suddenly leaned over and pushed her hands hard into Sarah's back. As Sarah whimpered, mother told Josie to "Get off her". Sarah moved towards the puzzle box but Josie whipped it away before she could reach it, muttering to herself, "Take it to the hall", which she did. As Sarah made to follow her, Josie grabbed her arm and squeezed it hard. Sarah cried out miserably and mother came to comfort her. As she sat down with Sarah on her lap, Josie shouted out, "Toilet mum!", so mum got up again to attend to Josie.

Although Josie enjoyed her game with Sarah, it was difficult for her to bear her sister having the exclusive attention of her mother during a feed and the close moments that followed. Josie may have felt pushed out, and she showed her feelings by squeezing Sarah so hard it was almost as if she was trying to make her disappear altogether.

## Juggling everyone's needs

Three-year-old Aneka and her friend Pete were trying to make a house outside and had climbed under the garden table to set up home. They needed a soft mattress and Aneka called to her mother to help. But mother told her not to interrupt while she fed the baby, so they crept upstairs to the parents' bedroom and lugged down their new white duvet, spreading it out on the muddy ground as a bed. They collected up all Aneka's dolls and laid them out on a corner of the duvet, where they began to "feed" them milk from their beakers. The feeding got increasingly messy and the "babies" were then given a rather rough hair-wash in the birdbath.

When their mother saw the milk and mud-stained duvet she was horrified and drew breath to yell at the children. She managed to control her fury, but talked to the children about how they had really spoilt something that didn't belong to them, making it quite clear how upset and disappointed she was. Aneka pleaded, "Don't tell Daddy", although her father had never been particularly harsh with her. Mother said that she didn't think it was a good idea to keep secrets from Daddy but that she was sure Daddy would not be too angry about it. She had a little weep indoors, and when her husband returned home they discussed how Aneka was clearly unable to manage her feelings about being excluded from the feeding mother and baby couple, and could not manage the burden of responsibility for her actions. Mother would have to ensure that Aneka received some attention too, and juggle the children's demands as best she could.

The parents could support each other and even see the humorous side of the children's play. If they weren't going to have mother's attention, then they would just have to *be* mother and father instead. That evening the subject came up again and father suggested that Aneka help him put the duvet in the washing machine. Aneka appeared relieved that she could do something to repair the damage, and that it was all out in the open. Her parents had been annoyed, but the fierce punishing father she was expecting had been proved to belong to her inner fantasy world. Mother and father had worked together to cope with an unpleasant but not too serious situation.

## Older siblings

For a three-year-old, having an older sibling can bring great rewards as well as heartache at times. It is true that they have many more skills than the young child, and this can be frustrating. It can, however, also be a spur to development, as the child tries to achieve some of her admired brother or sister's skills. If siblings are of the same sex, the rivalry may be more intense, because the older sibling may have felt more displaced by a same-sex baby at birth than otherwise, but equally over time they may have a lot in common. Tim learnt most of his football skills from his older brother Joe, who took great pride in teaching him how to dribble with the ball at an early age, and continued to show an interest in his sporting activities well into his school years. Joe's football team made Tim their mascot and he ran onto the field bursting with pride before each game. The age gap can also make a difference; children born just a year apart may seem more like equals, and tensions around sharing might be particularly high.

If there is a greater age gap the older sibling may flaunt such privileges as having a later bedtime or watching more grown-up television programmes. She may also help the younger child in many ways, teaching him new games from the playground, and introduce him to a range of older toys, older friends, junk food – she may also become annoyingly like a parent, enjoying her superior position of authority but sometimes lacking the sympathy and atten- tiveness that a parent brings to the relationship. If asked to help her younger sibling with a puzzle, she is likely to put the puzzle piece into its place rather than have the patience to help the child find the place himself. An older sibling is a mixed and rich package and the younger child has a very different experience of growing up from an only or the eldest child.

How they get on together depends on the temperaments of both children, how secure within herself and tolerant an older sibling is, or how much she feels the need to "put down" her baby brother or sister. This may depend on her own experience as a baby and whether her little girl or baby feelings have found acceptance with her parents. This would enable her to be more tolerant of a baby sibling. Parents can do a lot to help the sibling relationship along, by making sure they do not place too many demands on an older sibling to be "the responsible one", or to do too many chores for the younger child which could make her resentful. Taking care not to assume that the older sibling is always to blame can reduce the tension between them, as sometimes the younger sibling can be very good at provoking an older brother or sister and then letting him or her take the blame. "But she's only three, she doesn't know better!", is a cry that older siblings are probably quite allergic to. Complaints about sharing attention are common, with older siblings often feeling that the younger one gets more than his fair share.

Having a brother or sister can be fun and even though older siblings sometimes complain about their nuisance baby brother or sister following them around and copying everything they do, they often have a sense of great pride in their siblings and can be fiercely protective of them. Sometimes siblings enjoy "ganging up" mischievously as comrades against their parents, children against the adults.

When Ted had been sent upstairs without his ice-cream dessert for writing on the wall, Jenny, aged five, sneaked some chocolate upstairs for him instead. She could empathize with his situation. She and Ted always enjoyed playing on the beach together on holiday, when they didn't have other play-mates around. They spent most of one morning building a large sandcastle, Ted enjoying carrying the buckets of water to wet the sand, and Jenny deco-rating the walls with shells and a flag. When it was nearly done Ted said: "You and me live in the castle, Jenny. Mummy and Daddy must stay outside." "Yes," said Jenny enthusiastically, "we'll build a moat and they won't be able to come in unless we let them." The children were enjoying the power of being a sibling couple, and could play out together their shared mixed feelings about their parents as a couple who sometimes exclude the children.

They began building the moat, trickling the muddy brown sand from their fingers to form a wall. Ted laughed, "It's poo poo, look, coming out of your bum bum!" "No, it's yours! You still wear a nappy for your poos."

Ted looked away at the reminder of his difficulty with pooing in the toilet, but soon began giggling excitedly as Jenny joined him in making big "plops" of mud all over their castle.

At this age children are very interested in their bodily functions and waste products. Toilet humour and words connected to these areas can cause excite-ment and give rise to much giggling and amusement. Sometimes older siblings who might be "at each other's throats" can join forces against a third, often younger sibling.

Rivalry between Chris (three years) and Sue (18 months) was intense with constant fights breaking out between them, while six-month-old baby Harry watched with interest from his mother's lap. One day when Harry was asleep, their mother came upon the two children playing together at the doll's house with quiet concentration. To her amusement she saw that they had named the baby doll figure "Harry" and were enjoying pushing "Harry" head first down the toy toilet. They had buried their differences and joined forces to play at getting rid of the baby.

## Talking things over: conversations between friends

Parents need the companionship of other parents with whom to share their experiences, someone to lend a sympathetic ear, offer another point of view. Talking things over with a caring friend can help a parent sort things out in her own mind and this, in turn, can help a child to feel understood. This section charts the conversations between two friends over a few months focusing on three-year-old Max, and highlights some common delights and antics, worries and questions that concern many parents with young children around the time of a new baby's arrival.

We hear about Max's response to his mother's pregnancy as he tries to manage his worries about being excluded when the new baby arrives. Things aren't helped by the fact that the baby's due date falls close to Max's fourth birthday. We hear a detailed description of the birthday party and can picture Max's excitement and nervousness about sharing his presents and candle-blowing with a crowd of eager children. Questions arise about sexuality in young children – are they sexual beings? It can be useful to mull over these and many other issues with a friend.

Betty and Kate have been friends since school days and have always kept in touch. Betty lives in a small country village with her husband Guy and three-year-old Max; Kate, a single mum, lives in London with Pippa, also aged three, and baby Rob. They speak to or email each other regularly, to share their experiences of life with a three-year-old. Betty will soon be giving birth to her second child and is finding it tough going with three-year-old Max. The friends talk over the exciting but stressful period for Max and his family over the three-month period around the birth of their second child.

## The build-up to baby's arrival

Betty:     Last night Max watched us hauling out his Moses basket from the loft, then he disappeared into the living room where we heard a lot of banging and bumping around. It turned out he had pushed all the movable furniture around, rearranging the whole room. We left him to it (it's quite childproof), and when we returned a few minutes later we couldn't get in, he had barricaded the door and we were shut out! We started to panic a bit and eventually managed to squeeze in the door. What do you make of this?

Kate:    Do you think he was upset at seeing you getting his baby things out ready for the new baby? Perhaps it suddenly all began to feel very real. I remember you telling me that Max wouldn't look when you tried to show him the baby moving inside, so maybe he's been able to convince himself there's nothing really in there until now. When we got Pippa's pram out in preparation for Rob, she kicked it first, then climbed in and wanted to sleep the night there! I don't think she liked the idea of an empty pram just waiting for the next baby to take it over.

Betty:   That could be! In fact I remember now that we heard him making babbling baby sounds as we stood outside the living room door waiting for him to let us in.

Kate:    But what can we make of this rearranging the living room? It's a puzzle. The one thought that occurs to me is that he feels everything in his life is going to be rearranged by this baby. So, clever clogs, he reorganizes your room so that *you both* have to know what he feels like, you know, a bit confused and disorientated, unsure where his place is in the family. Ditto him shutting you out of the room, I mean his nose has been put out of joint by the fact that you've gone ahead and made a baby without his say so, and he sounds worried about whether he will be left out of things once the baby arrives. So, he shuts you both out of your own living room and you can see how *you* like it!

Betty:   Mm interesting... He sure lets us know how he's feeling. If what you're saying is true, and he is trying to make us feel how he feels by his behaviour, he must be pretty angry at the moment, because I seem to spend a lot of time feeling angry and upset with him. Do you think this is what he's trying to get across? To be honest, he is being such a handful at the moment I don't know how we are going to manage another one.

Getting out some of the baby equipment may well stir up mixed feelings for a three-year-old. She might need reassurance that she will not be forgotten or neglected. She may become interested in photos or video footage of herself as a baby, and ask endless questions about what she was like as a baby. From her point of view she cannot understand why her parents should possibly want another baby once they have had her. The period of anticipation before the baby arrives is often more stressful than after the birth. This may be because the uncertainty involved for all the family can be stressful, and often the child's imagination paints a worse picture of life with baby than the reality.

## Early waking

Betty: Yesterday was a typical morning and I have to admit I had shed a few tears by lunchtime.

Kate: What happened?

Betty: Well he woke at 6 o'clock which we've already established as too early for us and he sneaked into our bed for a cuddle. Then he insisted on following me into the loo and sitting on my lap as usual (he can hardly fit on and it is really uncomfortable!). I took him back to his room with instructions to play until 7 o'clock – you know he can read the clock in his room. He wanted me to play with him, I offered a kiss, and said I'd see him at 7 o'clock. He followed me into our room again, started butting his head against mine and trying to pull me out of bed to come back to his room... This went on until eventually, I took him out, closed the door, and fell back into bed. Guy hadn't stirred and I started to feel furious with him too!

Kate: Typical! But Betty, I couldn't *bear* having my child in the toilet with me, let alone sitting on my lap! I do think you're entitled to go to the loo in peace. Go on, I am sure he can manage, even if he does have a tantrum the first couple of times and bang on the door – get Guy to take him! I can see things from Max's point of view though – I mean it must feel unfair to him that the baby inside never has to separate from you, it just goes everywhere with you, including to the loo. Do you think that this is making him extra clingy at the moment? When I was pregnant Pippa used to pull up my dress and crawl underneath it for a cuddle, almost as if she wanted to get back inside again.

Betty:   I know you're right, it's just that I haven't got the energy to fight all these battles at once. (*The morning saga continues*) Max began banging on our door with a building brick demanding that I open it "now". I got up and told him that the banging made me angry and I'd leave the door open if he went and played in his room until 7 o'clock (only 15 minutes to go now). Eventually he went off and played for 10 minutes, then came to fetch me at 7 o'clock exactly. I was already exhausted.

## Angry attacks on parents

Betty:   We went downstairs and after an argument over his request for a *big* bottle of milk when we had agreed he would have a little one to leave space for breakfast, we went into the sitting room, Max with bottle, me with tea. I gave him his breakfast and took out some mending. He wandered over to see what I was up to and asked if he could help. I said he could cut the thread but that I'd like him to eat his breakfast first. He agreed but said he was taking the scissors back to the table with him. I ignored this and soon he came back over to see what he could cut. Before I had a chance to notice what he was doing, he had cut into the fabric of the waistcoat I was repairing for Guy. I was *so* angry! I mean honestly, is this normal?

Kate:   Listen, my friend, of course he's normal, he's having a bad time at the moment – this waiting period is tough, he's worried about how things will turn out, just as you probably are. I have a feeling he'll settle down once the baby has been born. At least Guy is under fire as well. I bet Max was imagining snipping off more than just a bit of his waistcoat! "Off with his willy" and he won't be making more babies, that's for sure. Anyway I think it's better that he gets some of his hostility out now and aims it at you two, rather than later at the baby.

Betty:   Thanks, that is a weight off my mind and I'm sure you're right, I just miss my lovely cuddly boy. Do you know, the other day he said in a very adult voice that he was sad to see that the *friendly mummy* had gone and that he could only see the *unfriendly one*. He asked me if I knew where she'd gone and I told him she had gone off with the friendly Max and that when he came back she might too…!

It is not only the older siblings who experience feelings of sadness at the imminent changes to family life – parents too feel guilt at what may be perceived as a betrayal of their older child, and may also fear rejection and exclusion. These intense feelings may be passed from one member of the family to another in the build-up to baby's arrival.

## Offloading feelings

Betty:  Well, to continue…I went upstairs to report to Guy, who came down and told Max how upset he was to hear about his waistcoat (which actually is old and not so important). He asked if it would be all right for him to cut up some of Max's clothes and Max protested loudly! Max pottered around downstairs while I got myself ready to take him to nursery. He seemed to be in quite a jolly mood, while I felt frazzled.

Kate:  I wonder if this proves the point I was making earlier about Max needing to unload some of his feelings into the two of you. Once he has managed to upset you both, and has got you to take his angry feelings on board, he seems to be in very good spirits.

Betty:  Yes, maybe, I could have strangled him, to be honest!… I called down to him to get his shoes on and reminded him to finish his breakfast, but he said he had had enough. I didn't make an issue of this to keep the food power game out of the equation. We headed out to the car after he'd said goodbye to Guy, who told him again how upset he was about his waistcoat. Max said, "Sorry I won't do it again" (we're not convinced) and added that he might cut burglars' clothes sometimes (he spends a lot of time in and out of story/fantasy worlds).

Kate:  Well, he seems to need someone to be the "baddy". Someone's got to be blamed for this turmoil in his life and he's using his imagination to play out some of his feelings.

Pippa regularly told me she was going to put me in handcuffs and send me to prison, so I think this is pretty standard fare.

Betty:   Well, Max is making it clear he has a very low opinion of me at the moment; the other day he told me I was "fired"! (*Laughter*).

## Going to nursery

Betty:   In the car I told Max that I wouldn't stay to do a puzzle with him as usual when we got to nursery because I was feeling so upset and angry with him. He complained but seemed to accept this. When we got to school he stayed belted in his seat, a bit subdued now. I opened his door, which made him furious and he slammed it shut again, eventually opening it himself. He got out and hit me with his jumper. Things continued in this manner, he refused to do anything I asked and he kicked me as we were walking into the classroom. I told him I would not tolerate that and that I would not even stay for a minute if he continued. I said that he could have a kiss and a hug and then I was going. He held on to me begging me to stay and do a puzzle. I reminded him why I wasn't in the mood for that, and offered him a last chance for a kiss. He gave in and made his way to the window to wave. I felt a little bad leaving him like that, because he looked so small and vulnerable as I left, but I find these endless negotiations so exhausting.

Kate:    It's funny isn't it? One minute they think they're running the show, the next they seem to need you so much. Do you think his refusals to do anything you asked might have been connected to your "refusal" to do the puzzle with him? I imagine that he actually felt quite worried, after all his attacks and banging at you, about whether you would come back to fetch him at all or just leave him there. That may be why he found it hard to let you go. It might be interesting to see what happens if you keep nursery and home separate and don't carry over behaviour from home to school – I think he might really need you and your comfort when he gets to school. When Rob was born Pippa insisted on bringing a toy mobile phone to nursery with her, just in case I didn't come and pick her up, then she could phone and remind me!

Betty: That does make sense, I must say. Perhaps he picked up my feeling that I was desperate for a break from him. The nursery staff say he's getting along fine at school, so he's obviously keeping the "good" Max for nursery and keeping the worst for home!

## Children's sexual feelings

Betty: Kate, I am beginning to wonder whether children of this age have a "sexual life" because Max definitely seems to have developed great "loves" – he talks a lot about a little girl called Rosemary at school, who has "shaky" (i.e. long) hair and he likes the TV presenter from *Hi-5*, Charli (very pretty with a friendly face and long blonde hair). He even named his baby doll Charli.

Kate: Well it's not surprising given that you have similar hair too, can't you see, he adores you?

Betty: Well yes, there may be something in that…he can be very loving to me, comes and strokes my hair and gives me slobbery kisses! But listen to this, one morning Max told me that Charli was the "beautifulest" – and I responded that "*I'd like to be the beautifulest*" – Max paused in thought and then said "how about you be the loveliest?" – which, I felt, all things considered (unwashed hair, old age etc.) was a pretty good offer! Do you think children have some sort of sexual feelings even at this age?

Kate: Well yes, I do. Don't you remember seeing Max having an erection when you were changing him as a baby? I remember that very well with my nephew Roger. After dealing with a girl, I got quite a surprise.

Betty: Now you say that, it reminds me of a funny incident when we were on holiday last summer. We had spent a day with Guy's nieces and nephews at an outdoor swimming pool – kids running round all day in costumes having lots of fun – Max had had a particularly nice time with a ten-year-old girl called

Jess who tried to teach him to swim. Max kept telling me afterwards how much he liked Jess and when I asked what it was he especially liked about Jess, he replied, "Her bosoms and her fanny"! I was a bit shocked I have to admit. I grew up with female genitalia being quite taboo and certainly the naming of them totally out of the question – so I try to be very open with Max about bodies but it was curious that he should think of a girl's body like that or am I reading too much into this?

Kate: We can't deny what we see and hear, can we? It certainly sounds as if his love for his gorgeous mother and his attraction to these lovely girls with 'shaky' hair are all mixed up into quite a potent cocktail for a three-year-old. At least someone's not noticing those bags under your eyes!

Betty: Well, his birthday party is happening soon, so I'm curious to see whether he asks me to invite Rosemary to come. He has already invited half the neighbourhood including our dentist. I think he feels this is his big chance to get into everyone's good books, especially the dentist (he wasn't brilliantly behaved last time we went).

It is difficult for parents to take on board that children experience sexual feelings and can be aroused by sensory stimuli such as touch and smell from infancy. It is common to see baby boys with an erection when they are being changed or bathed and little girls will often rub their genital area. However, the arousal is not necessarily focused on the genitals but excitement can be expressed through the mouth and oral activities and general levels of physical activity.

The inviting of all and sundry to Max's party is interesting, since the theme of exclusion is clearly foremost in his mind as the date for the new baby's arrival approaches. Max seems to feel identified with all the left-out people, and insists on including them. This is also his one opportunity to repair relationships if he feels he has been difficult around someone or to keep slightly scary people (e.g. dentist) sweet.

Three weeks later…

## The birthday party

Kate:     I'm so sorry we had to miss the party but Pippa still had spots from her chickenpox. Tell me all about it.

Betty:    Well, we did have to warn Max that if the baby decided to pop out we might choose a different day "very soon" to do the party…fortunately that didn't happen and we had fun with the preparations…but as for the actual party…it was a bit horrendous, to be honest!

Kate:     Too much of a build-up?

Betty:    Perhaps. It began with the presents. Max had suggested piling them up and opening them after the party (he'd seen it somewhere else). I said I thought it would be more exciting to open them straight away and say thank you and Max agreed. How I regret that decision now. His first present was an electric toothbrush.

Kate:     I bet he loved that.

Betty:    He was delighted with the next one, holsters and guns, and he began racing around with his friends shooting everything in sight! In the middle of this rampaging one of his quietest girl friends from nursery arrived, and was nearly knocked over. She began crying and clinging to her mother's skirt, refusing to let her leave. Another child began crying because Max and his "gang" were forcing him to be the "baddy" and threatening to put him in jail. Max thought Douglas was going to take his new guns home and pulled his hair…do you get the picture?

Kate:     Say no more!

Betty:    The last child arrived and we sat down to play pass the parcel, but they all looked a little glum and I began to worry that the atmosphere was not what I'd imagined. Perhaps I'd been too much of a cheapskate with the presents! A treasure hunt, a bit more running around, then I thought we were ready to eat, but Max looked tearful and refused to join us. In the end he reluctantly came to the table, but didn't eat much and kept returning to me for cuddles.

Kate:    It sounds as if he felt overwhelmed with excitement and perhaps he was a bit threatened by so many children all wanting to play with *his* toys. I wonder if he was feeling particularly sensitive about sharing on that day because he was worried that the new baby could arrive on his birthday and overshadow it – imagine having to share *his* birthday with a new baby.

Betty:    That makes sense, because sharing was definitely the problem. The last straw came with the cake. I called everyone in and Max told me he didn't want to share the cake, he was worried someone would blow out his candles. I said something sympathetic but ignored him: the cake was a labour of love in treasure chest design and I didn't stay up late decorating it for it to be left out of the proceedings! We lit the candles and sang "Happy Birthday", which Max complained he hadn't wanted and, thankfully, parents started arriving to collect their children. Max did a good job of saying goodbye (as if he couldn't wait for them to go) and insisted on giving the balloons out himself. He perked up as the crowd diminished and played contentedly with the last child, which made for a happier ending than seemed likely. Well, aren't you pleased you gave it a miss?

Kate:    It sounds tough on you all. I guess Max was finding it hard to share. I wonder whether it felt to him as if everyone was taking over his birthday when they sang "Happy Birthday"! I remember that a guest did blow out Pippa's candles last year and she was devastated. Do you think the fact that there is a new baby around might have made him extra sensitive around "birth days"? After all, the older he gets, the more he is making place for the new baby. I expect they'll all be older by next year and you'll have a better time of it!

Any event that doesn't form part of the child's ordinary routine, even the most pleasurable or exciting one, will be disruptive to a small child. Giving yourself plenty of time to prepare for the event, be it a holiday, a trip to the zoo or party, can increase the chances of a successful event. The build-up and anticipation of the occasion can sometimes eclipse the event itself, and if there are too many competing attractions a child may be overwhelmed, and become fractious. Being among big crowds, or stuffed into packed trains, can be frightening for small children and they need to feel secure that the adults are confident of their way and in control of the situation.

## The baby arrives

Kate:     Congratulations, well done! And to have had a girl as well, one of each! How is Max taking things?

Betty:     I must say, better than we had expected. He is very proud of her and the other day he told me he really had wanted a baby – it's almost as if he believes he is the father. He talks to her in a delightful imitation of adult baby talk: "little darling…you're so sweet…oh yes you are". And enjoys diagnosing whether she is tired, hungry or just needing a cuddle with her big brother. He does get angry with me sometimes, and luckily Guy has been around more to spend time with him. I dare say when he goes back to work things will get a bit tougher…still, he's got a few months to go before she can spoil his Lego models!

Kate:     It sounds as if he is relieved now that the baby has arrived, despite his lack of enthusiasm about the pregnancy. When Rob was born we tried to make a real fuss of Pippa, and gave her a present "from the baby" – a cassette tape player for her room, which went down well. By the way I have put two presents in the post, one for baby Jo and one for Max – his is a T-shirt saying, "I'm the *Big Brother*!" I hope he likes it.

Betty:     Thanks, that sounds perfect, as he likes the idea of being "Big Brother" and of Jo and him being a unit. He told me that he and Jo were in my "tummy" together and that they had an agreement that *he* would come out first! The other day he told me he knew *he* was right about something because Jo had told him when he was in my "tummy" with her. I guess they could grow into quite fearsome allies!

Kate:     Well, we all need allies in this world, I guess! I have really enjoyed talking to you, Betty, cheerio for now.

# 4

# Coping with Anger

## Anger and aggression

We all need to be aggressive to some extent, in order to survive. A healthy dose of assertiveness is a sign of character and determination, enabling a child or adult to move forward confidently in the world. Too much hostility which can get out of control is another matter, whether in the nursery play area or as adults in a bar. Small children can be filled with angry hostile feelings towards the most important people in their world, their parents, and later on, towards their friends and teachers and may imagine hurting or killing them off. The more aggressive their fantasies are, the more frightened they may become of monsters or other scary creatures which they fear may come and attack them back, especially when they are alone at night. Sometimes children cannot manage their own aggressive impulses and they bite, kick or hit out at other children. Over time and with help from the adults, children find ways of expressing their feelings through play and eventually talking about them. They may use imaginary weapons, sticks for guns, toy swords, toy animals or whatever comes to hand to play out these feelings.

Mark was playing near his younger sister Lucy, who sat with her back to him, building a castle with mother. He picked up a toy crocodile and, opening and closing its jaws, he made snapping sounds with his mouth. He made the crocodile "bite" into the back of Lucy's dress. Mother told him to stop hurting his sister, and suggested he play with his toy animals. He took out all the piglets from his farm set, and the mother kangaroo with a baby kangaroo in her pouch. He made the crocodile lock its jaw around the baby animals one by one and drop them from the table onto the floor where Mark pronounced them "all dead". The last to "die" was the baby kangaroo and the crocodile tugged him out of the mummy kangaroo's pouch, munched on him a few times, then tossed him down with the others. His mother looked over, occasionally exclaiming, "Those poor baby animals are really getting a rough time."

Once he was stopped from actually hurting his sister, Mark went and played out some of his aggressive feelings towards her. Although she may have been rather shocked at the violence of his play, Mark's mother did not overreact or stop him but showed some interest in the play. Given the opportunity to express some of their fantasies through play, in a safe containing environment, children are less likely to cause hurt or damage to others.

Over dinner Mark seemed a bit subdued and he asked his parents: "Do crocodiles eat grass for dinner? I think they do." He probably knew in a part of him that crocodiles eat meat (even humans), but this idea was too frightening to him, considering his play earlier in the day, so he calmed things down by turning crocodiles into vegetarians.

## Excessive aggression

Sometimes children become excessively aggressive, attacking their parents, wrecking toys and hurting other children. Parents may feel their three-year-old is out of their control. In these cases they may seek help from a specialist service for families with children under five. When we meet these families we often discover that the problems have existed for a long time. If, for some reason, a mother was depressed or preoccupied with other problems, she may not have been able to be 'there' for her baby, to think about his changing needs in the ordinary way mothers do. Some babies can be difficult to attend to, always fussing and never satisfied. This uneasy relationship sometimes leads babies to become "super-independent", developing their physical skills so they can get around without help. They may also get into the habit of having to scream or cry that bit louder, kick that bit harder if they want to attract their mother's attention and get through to her. This attention-attracting behaviour may carry on into toddler-hood as the child expects he will have to kick up quite a fuss before his needs are attended to. This sometimes accounts for the hyperactive and aggressive behaviour one sees in some young children. It may not always be possible for parents to sort out these difficulties on their own and they may seek help at their local child mental health clinic, which is what Pansek's parents did when they became concerned about his aggression towards his mother.

Pansek had had a difficult start to life; his mother's own mother had become ill and died during the pregnancy. The delivery was difficult and Pansek did not take easily to the breast. There was little support from extended family members, who lived some distance away. Mother missed her own mother and became sad and depressed during the first difficult months. She found it hard to bear Pansek's crying, moving away to another room and leaving him to scream for long periods. The parents didn't always agree on how to manage him and this led to arguments. Pansek developed physically very fast, and was walking by eight months. In fact he always seemed to be on the go and rarely asked for help, dressing and feeding himself before he was two years old. He became fascinated with motorbikes like his father, and swaggered around the house wearing father's large bike helmet looking as if he was armed against all danger.

He had huge tantrums, kicking and hitting out at his mother whenever she set any limits. The more he attacked her, the more of a failure she felt as a mother, and she confided in a friend that she only enjoyed being with Pansek when he was sick or sleepy because she felt needed when he cuddled up to her. It seemed as if Pansek's way of coping with his early worries and disappointments had been to give up on his baby needs and develop a tough bullying exterior.

He was well defended against disappointment, determined not to show his needs. Since the parents had difficulty supporting each other in setting limits for Pansek, he got the message that no one could stop him from doing whatever he wanted to do. This may have made him feel unsafe, leading him to become even wilder at home, because constant activity was his way of managing his anxiety. He also began treating their new puppy cruelly, kicking it at every opportunity. Perhaps the puppy stood for a baby in Pansek's mind. Around this time Pansek developed a terror of flies and bees, and the sound of buzzing sent him scurrying indoors. Could this fear be connected to all his attacks on his mother? Perhaps Pansek imagined that through his aggression he had done some damage to her and to her unborn babies; now he feared that they were all buzzing angrily at him, waiting to attack him back.

Work with the whole family took place to think with them about the meaning of Pansek's anxieties, and how as parents they could cooperate together to help him feel more contained.

## Temper tantrums

Although there is a lot of talk about the "terrible twos", there is no magic cut-off point at a child's third birthday, especially when it comes to a child expressing passionate feelings of excitement, fear or fury. Everyone gets angry sometimes, and learning how to express angry feelings is an important part of children's development. Small children can feel quickly overwhelmed by intense rage if, for example, a parent refuses them something or stops an activity and they cannot always put these feelings into words. The only way they can cope is to get rid of these feelings, by kicking, biting, screaming, spitting. It is as if with each kick or scream they are pushing out the awful feelings.

Sometimes a child has a tantrum in a busy supermarket or shoe shop, and parents feel embarrassed and humiliated, especially if they lose their cool and shout back at their child or even hit him. At these moments children may imagine their own anger is so powerful and dangerous that it can actually do real damage, for example, cause harm to frustrating parents or siblings. It is important for children to know that their angry outbursts may *feel* as if they're dangerous, but are not really so, nor are they necessarily too much for the adults to handle. A child's unconscious aim may be to make a parent feel the anger he (the child) is experiencing at that moment and he may increase the force of his screams and kicks until his parents acknowledge how angry he is feeling. Of course sometimes a child is already beyond hearing or *taking in* anything anyone might say, so concentrated is he on getting feelings *out* of himself. He may simply need his parents to stay nearby, absorbing the powerful feelings that are coming their way, or holding him, but without necessarily saying much.

Weathering a tantrum is a bit like going through a storm on a ship; it feels scary and dangerous but just has to be endured. Saying "No" to a child is a basic and essential part of parenting, and learning how to deal with the frustration of his parents saying "No" is an important part of a child's development. Parents sometimes come to the clinic concerned because their small children are "out of control", and they are having difficulty setting limits. It may turn out that parents have come from families where discipline was severe and harsh, and are determined not to repeat this with their own children. Others may have had a very "liberated" childhood with few rules imposed and are reluctant to set firm boundaries, organize their children into a routine, or agree on consistent approaches.

## Saying "No"

Children can make their parents feel that they are being cruel and unreasonable when they say "No". They feel guilty and bad for depriving their child of something and sometimes worry that frustrating a child in this way could be harmful, even if they know in a part of themselves that their refusal has been reasonable and necessary. This makes it difficult for them to say "No" as if they really mean it. Children pick up whether a parent is really serious about their refusal or prohibition. They also pick up whether parents are not in agreement with each other.

Sometimes parents feel they have to give a reasoned logical explanation for saying "No". It may be helpful for them to realize that they are not harming their child by saying "No" and setting firm limits; on the contrary, clear boundaries can help children to feel safe and contained. Children can become quite worried if they feel that they can do whatever they want to, and that no one can stop them. It gives them the illusion of being all powerful, but also makes them feel unsafe, because if their parents are unable to stop them, and to protect themselves or their home from attack, how will they be able to keep a child safe? This can lead to a vicious cycle where a child becomes more and more overactive, increasingly pushing at the boundaries, to test whether and when the adults will finally stop him. Parents are sometimes surprised and gratified when their child calms down quickly and appears to be relieved when stopped. He can drop the big powerful "tough guy" act, and show some chinks in his armour, show some younger, more vulnerable feelings, worries and fears, knowing that he will be kept safe by his parents, who recognize his limits. If they are very upset children may not be in the right frame of mind to take in explanations or to understand them. They also need to know that some things are forbidden, simply because their parents say so.

However, deciding when to say "No" can be a challenge to parents. Three-year-olds can be very strong-willed, they are curious and love to explore their environment. They are interested in how things work, particularly gadgets that their parents are fond of using, such as the mobile phone, Daddy's razor, Mummy's hairdryer or laptop. Many objects look attractive to touch, eat, feel, and children need to be offered a sense that on the whole the world is a safe and interesting place. We don't want to fill our children with anxiety about too many risks, or crush their determination and enthusiasm, but we do need to ensure that they know about the dangers of road traffic, stoves, fires etc. In situations where there is a risk of real danger or damage to property, the parents' position is clear cut, but in day-to-day life parents will be faced with many "grey areas", and they may have to weigh up which battles are worth fighting and where there can be a bit of leeway.

It seems important to be consistent, so that a child knows what the limits are, but there may also need to be room for manoeuvre. For example, if a child is unwell he may need to be close to his parents and sleep in their bed for a few nights. Parents then have the tricky task of deciding at what point he is well enough to return to his own bed, and stand firm despite protests. They may have a rule about no ice cream before a meal, but if a child has just had an injection at the doctor's, or been to the station to say goodbye to a much loved grandparent, there may be room for compromise.

## Bribery and threats

Every parent at some time or other has promised their child a toy, a sweet, if they will just be good at the shops, or sit quietly during a meeting. What is the difference between offering a delayed treat after a stressful time, and bribery? The difference may lie in whether it is the parent who retains control over the situation and makes the decision based on an understanding of the child's needs, or whether it is the child who takes charge. If a child is told he is going to the dentist to make sure his teeth stay healthy, and that afterwards there will be a treat at McDonald's, he may have something to look forward to to help him manage his experience. If he senses that the decision is *his* and that his mother will do anything to get him to agree to go, he feels very powerful and might exert his control to demand more and more. He may also lose sight of the fact that mother is in charge, and although the visit could be unpleasant, it is being done in his best interests. Threats are the other side of the coin to bribery, both using the "if you do this/don't do this then I will/won't do that" formulation, based on a struggle for power rather than a focus on the child's needs. Threats can frighten a child so badly that he may lose his ability to do things properly and get into more trouble, or he may comply out of fear rather than in a spirit of cooperation. It is easy to fall into the trap of making a threat that we cannot carry out, for example, to cancel a child's birthday party – highly unlikely considering the practicalities. Children as young as three have excellent memories and might quickly learn that parents do not follow through on their threats. Threats of violence can terrify children and may lead them to become unnaturally subdued and "good".

Threatening to abandon a child or to send him away can backfire. A mother sat with her small child waiting for an X-ray at a large teaching hospital. Her daughter became restless, and asked first for "books" then for "water" and finally began jumping from one chair to another in boredom. Her mother said, "If you don't stop, I'm going to take you up to the ward and leave you there!" The little girl looked frightened and protested, "No!" She stopped jumping around and sat in subdued silence for another half an hour.

If at some later stage this child might need to go to hospital, she could have a picture in her mind of a hospital being a scary place where she could be left behind on her own as a punishment for her "naughtiness". Similarly, parents who threaten to leave a child behind at the childminder or the shops if they misbehave could be storing up trouble for later, when they are trying to settle a child in to nursery, as she will always have some worry that unless she is impeccably behaved, she could be left there.

## Smacking

Occasionally a parent will lose control and slap a child, particularly if he has done something dangerous. Grace watched horrified as her daughter Beth ran out into a busy street before she could stop her. Grace raced across the road, grabbed Beth and slapped her hard, screaming angrily at her. Then she burst into tears. She was overcome by the shock of what had happened and had lost control.

The way parents discipline their children depends a lot on the experience they had as children themselves, and what kinds of expectations their parents placed on them. Some parents still recall their fear of physical punishment and are determined not to subject their children to the same experience. Others feel that they have come to no harm and intend to do the same to their children, to make sure they toe the line. Many argue that they preferred a "good hiding" because "then it's over", rather than having to suffer a period of parental disapproval and anger. Enduring the brief physical pain seemed easier than having to think about the emotional distress of the incident.

Since children use their parents' behaviour as a model for their own, it is likely that a child who is regularly hit will react in a similar way when frustrated or angry. He will not have had the experience of a parent who has been able to talk to him about what he has done, or who has tried to understand what his behaviour means. Although we often have to act immediately to stop a child doing something dangerous or damaging, this doesn't mean we need to give up on trying to put ourselves into his shoes to understand what he might have been feeling or thinking about at the time.

Smacking a child as a regular form of discipline is not advisable. Children behave themselves out of fear rather than because they wish to please an admired parent. They may become subdued and timid and learn to be deceptive, committing sneaky acts of defiance. These often include inflicting hurt on younger children in identification with their punitive parent. Adults sometimes suggest, "Bite back if he bites you – then he'll see how it feels and won't do it again!" But hitting, kicking or biting a child back simply brings a parent down to the child's level and doesn't leave any room for thinking about the reason for a child's behaviour. The parent simply pushes all of the child's feelings back into him, filling him with even more angry feelings which, in turn, he attempts to push away. It is up to the parent to break the vicious cycle by trying to understand what the child is trying to express.

Oscar and his mother were both struggling with their feelings of anger and upset since Oscar's father had left the family three weeks before. His mother was feeling exhausted and irritable and Oscar became increasingly wild, jumping on the furniture and throwing pieces of his tea set at her. When she finally took the tea set away, Oscar flew into an uncontrollable rage, lunging at his mother and biting her hand. Overwhelmed with anger, mother hit him. The angry feelings had spiralled out of control and were bouncing back and forth between them. At that moment Oscar tumbled off the sofa and lay in a heap sobbing miserably. As he lay there crying, something about his smallness and vulnerability made mother's anger slowly drain away. She was reminded that he was still a young child who needed her more than ever at this time, in spite of his show of "toughness". She took him on her lap where he sobbed a long time, able at last to express the feelings of sadness and loss he had kept control over for so long.

# 5

# Working Things Out

## Toilet matters

Many children aged three are clean and dry, but may still have accidents from time to time. Children who usually manage perfectly well can regress at certain times, which is perfectly normal, for example, when a new baby is born. They may ask for a nappy "like the baby" or wet the bed. The less fuss is made about this the better, as in time they will revert to using the toilet as before. Some parents joke that if their children are capable of running to fetch their own nappy, they're old enough to use the toilet. It takes time before children can manage the whole process of toileting on their own. The cry "Come and wipe my bottom!" may be heard for a long time in some households.

Any change in routine, such as going on holiday, a brief separation from parents, moving house or a bad cold, can result in a child soiling or wetting the bed until he has settled into the new setting. Three-year-old Adam had been toilet-trained for a few weeks and was due to spend the night with his aunt. When she arrived he greeted her with "Hi poo poo!" and burst out laughing. For the next five minutes his entire conversation was punctuated with "poo poo" words, accompanied with much laughter. His mother and aunt talked about it and thought that perhaps Adam was feeling a little insecure about sleeping out and whether he would manage the toilet. He seemed to be testing out whether an "accident" with his poos as well as poo talk would be acceptable to his aunt.

As the time for going to playgroup or nursery approaches, parents whose children are not completely toilet-trained become worried that their child's entry may be delayed, since many nurseries insist on children being fully toilet-trained. It is probably best to keep the pressure off, trying to remain as relaxed and encouraging as possible. Where children are put under too great pressure they can become over-worried about cleanliness, afraid to get their clothes dirty with paint or play in the sand. They can become passive, observing others rather than joining in, for fear they might mess up their clothes or hair.

If a child who has been clean and dry for some time begins to wet or soil, there may be an underlying reason, usually some anxiety which might take time to work out. A child might be feeling the strain of being a big brave girl, letting her mother leave her at nursery each day, but when she is asleep and that control is relaxed, her worries stream out of her along with her urine. Her parents may be going through a rough patch in their marriage and she may be hearing more shouting at home than usual. Children pick up on tension at home and wetting, during the day or at night, can be a common response to stress. Sometimes parents find it helpful to attend a counselling service for small children, to get some help thinking about what might underlie this change in a child.

Some children may be fine about using the toilet for wees but may demand a nappy to poo into. There may be different reasons for this. Children can feel afraid of falling into the toilet or get frightened by the sound of the poo falling out of them into the pan below. It may feel as if they are losing a part of their body and they may hate the noise of the toilet flushing it away. The tight fit of the nappy can give them the illusion that the poo is still there as part of them. They may have a particular ritual attached to doing a poo. Stephen would ask for a nappy, go into his Daddy's study and leaf through one of his work books. He needed to feel like a grown-up man in his "top half" and could almost forget that down at the bottom a more baby-like activity was occurring. Poos can also be seen as precious treasures, gifts to parents, who always seem so delighted when they deliver the goods into the potty or toilet. At this age children are very interested in their bodily functions and waste products. Faeces and urine take on, in their fantasy, many magical powers. Children can imagine their faeces to be powerful weapons for example, to bomb enemies with. Johnny would sit on his potty and make the same kind of noises while pooing as he did when playing with his soldiers and guns. "Bang, bang, whiz, bomb", he would go, showing how much he linked his "plops" (his name for faeces) with dangerous weapons.

Urine too can be seen as a means of spoiling or damaging things, and children may deliberately wee on the carpet, their parents' bed or other household furniture as a sign of angry protest.

Maeve's mum was going to be away from home for a few days and her parents had explained that her best friend's mother would be picking her up from nursery and looking after her until her father collected her at the end of the day. Her father had promised to take her to the zoo as a special treat over the weekend. The day before her mother was leaving, Maeve was watching her Teletubbies video in the living room when she saw mother's overnight bag lying half open on the floor. She pulled it open, scattered out the contents and weed inside the case. She called out gleefully, "I'm doing a wee wee" and her mother came running to discover the damage. Maeve had given her mother an experience of what it felt like to have things messed up and spoilt for her.

## Relaxation and sleeping

Young children need a time and space at the end of the day with an adult they know well, to "chew over" some of the day's events in a relaxed way. They need to be given the opportunity to recall the day and its activities, but at their own pace and with parents following their lead and train of thought. This is quite different from the kind of pressure they may feel in front of visitors (or down the telephone) when they are encouraged to "tell Auntie Pam what you saw at the zoo and where you are going tomorrow". Parents might be surprised at what a child has taken in from an outing, and conversations at a quiet time often show what is really on a child's mind. She may have been excited and a bit frightened by going into the "car washing machine" (carwash) or she could have noticed a cat jumping across the rooftops and might suddenly ask, "Where are her babies?"

A.A. Milne in *Winnie-the-Pooh* captures this moment of quiet reflection when Christopher Robin is talking to Pooh Bear in the bath, after their adventure with the bees that afternoon. Pooh Bear, who had been floating near a bees' nest in a tree by hanging onto a balloon, had become desperate to get the balloon back on the ground to escape being stung. He had asked Christopher Robin to shoot it down but Christopher's first shot had missed the balloon and hit his friend instead. Christopher Robin now had a chance to reflect on the events of the day, and to talk to Pooh Bear about it, proving the point that telling an adventure to someone over again turns it into a real story, rather than merely a remembered account. Christopher Robin was able to voice his real concern that he might have hurt his friend when he fired his gun so inaccurately. Winnie the Pooh reassures him that he did not, and he is able to go to bed with peace of mind, which will ensure a good night's sleep.

## Storybooks and working through experiences

Illustrated storybooks are an excellent way for parents to spend time together quietly with their children, perhaps towards the end of a tiring day. In this age when even young children spend some time in front of screens, this form of interaction seems to be especially precious. Children's books explore important themes in a light humorous way and can form a focus for discussion and deep enjoyment. They are often beautifully observed and illustrated. Some stories are based on simple household activities, like *Doing the Washing* or *Going Shopping* by Sarah Garland. Others imaginatively explore the child's inner world: *Angry Arthur* by Hiawyn Oram and Satoshi Kitamura (illustrator) describes how a child imagines his angry feelings are so powerful they can destroy the universe. *Not Now Bernard* by David McKee shows Bernard attempting unsuccessfully to catch his busy parents' attention. They finally notice him when he turns into a monster – an image of how furious he has become by this stage and how wild he has to be before anyone takes notice of him. *Little Monster Did It!* by Helen Cooper touches on the child's need to separate out his "monster" from his "good boy" side. Whenever something naughty happens, it is always attributed to "monster". *Where the Wild Things Are* by Maurice Sendak puts into words those "wild", angry feelings inside that children may not be able to name. *Gorilla* by Anthony Browne evokes the fantasy and dream world of small children. Hannah's father is too busy to play with her. Her disappointment at the small toy gorilla he has bought her is transformed into joy during a dream sequence where the gorilla/Daddy sweeps her off on a series of treats and adventures. Mother is not mentioned and the sequence of the two of them dancing on the lawn together touches on issues relating to a young girl's wishes to be the special person in Daddy's life.

Many books describe the everyday struggles of small children: *New Clothes for Alex* by Mary Dickinson describes how Alex ends up buying the identical clothes he has outgrown, but one size bigger. This touches on a child's love of sameness: children often insist on wearing clothes they are particularly fond of until they are just about falling apart. In *You'll Soon Grow into*

*Them, Titch* by Pat Hutchins, the focus is on the child's position in the family; as the youngest child Titch inherits all the hand-me-downs from his older siblings. *The Bad-tempered Ladybird* by Eric Carle describes a ladybird, full of bravado, who picks a fight with bigger and stronger animals than himself. Carle's *The Mixed-up Chameleon* and *Do You Want to be my Friend?* focus on issues of identity and anxieties about friendship. *Mrs Lather's Laundry* by Allan Ahlberg and André Amstutz (illustrator) shows children involved in their parents' work lives and is humorous without poking fun at adults. *The Very Hungry Caterpillar* by Eric Carle combines the simplicity of a book for younger children with the complex concept of transformation from chrysalis to butterfly, as well as counting and days of the week.

Rhyming books which children memorize and where they can anticipate the next line are good preparation for reading, for example *All Join In* by Quentin Blake and *Each Peach Pear Plum* by Janet and Allan Ahlberg. Many books focus on particular issues, such as food fads, e.g. *Oliver's Vegetables* by Vivian French; toilet concerns, e.g. *I Want my Potty!* by Tony Ross; friendship issues, e.g. *I'm Not your Friend* by Sam McBratney; bedtimes, e.g. *Can't You Sleep, Little Bear?* by Martin Waddell and Barbara Firth (illustrator). Fairy tales have an enduring appeal although some can be too frightening for small children.

Finally, a story that might be just the thing for a tired parent at the end of a busy child-centred day and which can help a small child to identify with her parent: the enduring Jill Murphy book, *Five Minutes' Peace*, which shows the mother elephant's futile efforts to grab five uninterrupted minutes in the bath.

## Bedtime rituals

Small children need rituals to help them feel in control, especially at bedtime. Parents can stick to bedtime rituals even in the most unusual situations, and they offer a familiar routine in a strange setting. Bonnie's father always sang her a particular song accompanied by a drumming on the end of her bed. On their way to France they ended up sharing a couchette with two other people, and despite embarrassment, her father sang her the song, complete with the accompaniment.

## Sleeping difficulties

### Interrupting the parents

I discussed earlier children's Oedipal wishes towards their parents, and how this may affect their sleep. They have mixed feelings about their parents' intimate relationship and may not take kindly to being "put away to bed" so that their parents can enjoy an evening together. They might wander into the living room during the evening or wake to "check" on them during the night, crawling into their parents' bed and falling asleep there unless they are firmly returned to their bed. Parents may sometimes feel too exhausted to fight that battle and give in, often spending an uncomfortable cramped night. Or the game of "musical beds" gets going and one parent leaves to occupy the child's vacant bed.

Most children settle down to a regular pattern of sleep during the night, and younger three-year-olds may still be having a nap during the day. Some children will by temperament need less sleep and keep on the go longer than others. But you can guarantee that by the time they're 16 they'll be sleeping until noon at the weekend and parents will find themselves struggling to rouse their offspring.

### Letting go

Many children go through periods when their sleep is disrupted, and, often, as with bed-wetting or soiling, the underlying reason may be emotional. In particular it may link to worries in the child and parent to do with separation from each other. Night-time is often a time when children feel more vulnerable. The daytime runabout, full of bravado, may become more needy and baby-like at night. It is not an accident that the phrase "falling asleep" is used, because in a way one does need to "fall" into sleep and this implies a separation from and letting go of familiar figures to the child. This is why bedtime rituals are so important as they help parents and children make the transition and give a formal pattern to the separation from each other at the end of the day.

Parents often describe a child stringing out bedtime, calling down for "one last kiss" or a drink of water, clearly finding it difficult to let go of them. The dark can suddenly feel unfriendly and threatening, the chair placed at a certain angle may look like a person, and various checks and rearrangements might be necessary before a child can relax and go to sleep. Being kind but firm usually works in the end, although whenever there has been a break in routine, through illness, holiday or house move, for example, parents can expect that children will take longer to settle down.

## Picking up on worries

If parents are feeling anxious, upset or preoccupied with something else, even an exciting family reunion for example, a child may pick up on this and become more wakeful at night. Children often wake more when their mothers return to work and may react too if they increase their hours of work. A change of childminder or nursery key worker may also unsettle children. There is less likelihood of them having a disturbed night if they have had an opportunity at the close of day to talk over their day's activities. The matters that may be preoccupying them will probably emerge and there will be a chance to discuss their fears, worries or excited anticipation. Children can become overwhelmed with excitement for several nights before a holiday, birthday or Christmas and find it difficult to sleep or they may wake early.

## Night-time fears

Children often fear the dark and in their imagination familiar objects turn into frightening witches, wolves or ghosts. They may come into their parents' bed during the night for comfort. Although parents may feel cruel taking a frightened child back to her room, if they simply allow her to return to their bed night after night, the child might begin to believe that her parents share her night-time fears. Perhaps they too believe that sleeping on one's own is unsafe, that there really are dangerous creatures out there. She needs assurance that her imaginary fears are taken seriously but are not confirmed as real dangers from which she needs adult protection through the night.

## Dreams and nightmares

Children become aware of having had a dream in the night from around the age of two and will occasionally wake up in the morning saying they had a dream. They may not be able to say much about it as it may be more a swirl of impressions and images than a sequence of events. More often children wake up screaming because they have had a nightmare. They may feel the nightmare is "real" and need someone to take them out of their bedroom and calm them down. Sometimes the child will need to tell a parent there and then what the bad dream was about, and may be reluctant to go back to her own room. If a child has been particularly aggressive during the day, she may wake up having had a nightmare in which her aggressive actions of the day are transformed into vengeful figures, monsters or "baddies" from a TV programme who may come after her seeking revenge.

Billy had become very angry with his mother when she made him come in from the garden for his bath. He had screamed, "I hate you!" and had thrown his wellington boot in her direction. After his bath he watched the video of the story *The Three Little Pigs*. That night he woke up screaming, "Help, wolf bite me!" The wolf in his dream had managed to get right inside the house, and after his hostility to his mother he didn't feel very safe even in his "brick and cement" house.

If children are having nightmares, parents may need to be on the lookout for videos and television programmes that can alarm children, even though they are billed as suitable. We cannot assume that children will turn off the video or run out of the room if they're frightened. Sometimes they will, but they may also try to conquer their fear by watching the sequence over and over as if to try to get used to it. They sit transfixed, and if you look closely you may see that their fists are clenched and they are frozen with fear, but they watch on until the bitter end. We cannot entirely protect our children from frightening images and we may not always be able to predict what might be scary but some shows billed for children, e.g. some pantomimes and puppet shows, can be too much. If children are badly frightened they may be put off going to the theatre in the future, and it may be as well to check out the content of the show in some detail beforehand.

Children absorb far more than we realize from TV and the radio. Many parents sat horrified as they watched the events of 9/11 unfold on their television screens, with their small children playing nearby. They described their shock when children began playing out the horrific scenes by building brick towers and crashing them down accompanied by screams. Many children suffered from nightmares linked to witnessing the scenes on screen.

Children can have nightmares which may resemble flashbacks if they have been involved in a traumatic event, a car accident, fire or other disaster and parents may need to seek advice as to how best to help with these.

## Night terrors

Sometimes the terror stirred up in a child's nightmare is so powerful that it transfers onto usually familiar and friendly figures, of whom the child then appears to be terrified. Children having a night terror appear to be awake but are still in the grip of a trance-like state, and it may take some time before they emerge.

Gail had just arrived with her parents at the caravan park near the sea after a tiring day of car travel. This was her first time in a caravan and Gail obstinately refused to go with mum into the tiny bathroom to clean her teeth. Eventually mother lost her temper and shouted at her. Finally they settled down to read a new storybook, *Meg's Eggs* (by Helen Nicoll and Jan Pieńkowski), which featured a large dinosaur baby hatching out of a gigantic egg. Her parents were woken in the night by a scream of terror. Gail was sitting up but didn't seem to recognize them. Her mother approached to hand her a beaker of water, but Gail threw the beaker across the room, shouting in fear whenever her mother got too near. Her parents were concerned that she was ill, and hoped she would recover by morning.

However, in the morning Gail still seemed to be in a trance, and looked at mother fearfully as if she were a witch. Father was the only person allowed near her and he took her for a walk along the beach. Suddenly Gail said "Mummy...dinosaur...baby", which gave father a clue as to what might have set off the night terror. The long day of travel and the disorientation of unfamiliar surroundings must have contributed to Gail's unsettled sleep. The story about a witch (Meg) who gave birth to a "monster baby" (the dinosaur) seemed linked to Gail's own difficult, "monster" behaviour and her mother's "witch-y" shouting just before she went to sleep. These all seemed to get mixed up into a terrifying concoction, resulting in the "night terror". Gail seemed to have become "stuck" inside her nightmare, and so it looked as if mother *was really* the bad witch.

## Food fads and concerns around eating

Issues to do with food and feeding stir up strong emotions in most of us, since they are associated with many of our earliest experiences. The kind of relationship a child has to food is intimately connected to her early feeding experience with mother. If the mother–baby couple got off to a good start with the breast or bottle and the weaning to solid food went reasonably smoothly, by the time a child is three she will have her favourite foods but will be curious to try out new food on offer. Things do not always happen in this way and feeding difficulties often have an emotional basis: some babies may not have recovered from the loss of the bottle or breast, especially if weaning happened quickly. They may try to hold on to that early feeding stage by sticking to baby-like foods, milk or runny yoghurt and resisting chewy or lumpy food.

Some babies may have found it too difficult to wait for a feed and turned away from mother, learning how to hold a bottle on their own from a young age. These children may have difficulty allowing themselves to be fed any baby-looking food, but may go for finger food that they can hold on their own. We know how hurtful it can feel when children reject mother's carefully prepared home-cooked meals, but this is often a short-lived phase. In extreme cases children may reject all home-prepared food in favour of packaged or tinned products. This may be a sign of underlying emotional difficulties between mother and child, and help from a counselling service for families with young children could be sought.

Some children have worries (unconscious usually) about using their teeth for biting into hard foods, because they may connect teeth with strong wishes to hurt or attack others through biting. Teeth are the first weapons a child develops and children biting other children at nursery is a common complaint. Children going through this phase may also go off hard foods for a while.

Overeating in children can cause concern, and this too may stem from a child's early experiences at the breast or bottle. Perhaps she was given a bottle as a matter of course, whenever she cried, before anyone had worked out what her crying was about. She might have begun to expect a feed not only to relieve her hunger but also to quiet or comfort her. In this way she would want to eat whenever she felt a bit lonely, frightened or empty inside. These children often get labelled as "greedy" at nursery and may need help to sort out different needs and to recognize the many other ways there are to gain comfort and satisfaction.

Most children enjoy a reasonable range of foods although the nutritional combinations may not always be to our taste. As with toileting, a change in routine, a special event, or separation from parents may affect children's eating. Mary ate heartily at home but when she started going to nursery for the full day, she hardly touched her lunch. In fact she vomited for two days in a row as soon as she sat down at the table she shared with eight other children. It was almost as if she was physically getting rid of an upsetting emotional experience. Her mother wondered, with nursery staff, whether Mary found mealtimes at nursery overwhelming, a time when she missed the close one-to-one contact with her mother. They decided to go back to half-day attendance for a month and then see how things settled down. By that time Mary had found a friend whom she sat next to, which enabled her to manage mealtimes at nursery.

## Picky eaters

Although your three-year-old child may have already developed strong likes and dislikes, it helps to continue offering an expanded range of foods, giving some (limited) choices because children can be unpredictable in what they fancy. They may appear to be committed to a sweetcorn and rice cakes diet forever, then suddenly decide to try something new one day and like it. The Dr Seuss book, *Green Eggs and Ham*, where Sam is urged to "try it, try it and you may (like it)", captures some children's reluctance to try new things and the eventual rewards if they do.

## Junk food

Concerns are growing about the amount of "junk food" consumed by small children, because of worries about their teeth, obesity and hyperactivity. Patterns of eating are established early in life and if a child gets used to eating healthily she will be less at risk of obesity and its related health hazards. First or only children are often protected by parents from exposure to chocolate and sugary drinks at a young age, but once there is an older sibling in the house, one can be sure that a child will have tried and tested most junk foods by the time she is three. The barrage of advertisements for foods high in salt, fat and sugar makes the parent's task of limiting the child's intake more difficult.

This is an area where working out together how and when to say "No" would be an important task for parents, since children will enjoy wangling an extra chocolate biscuit out of one parent when refused by the other. Parents realize quickly that although they can control what the child eats at home or when she's out with them, life can become pretty miserable if they try to exert too much control over what she eats when with others. It can put a child in an awkward position to have to refuse an ice cream before lunch if offered at a friend's house, and can also make a child feel as if she has cheated and triumphed over her parents and their rules if she accepts.

Parents of children who for health (e.g. diabetic) or religious reasons have to exclude some foods from their diet usually speak to the parents of friends or teachers to make sure that the adults know what a child is allowed, or can provide alternatives so that the child is not burdened with having to use her own self-control when surrounded by friends all eating what they choose.

## Links with behaviour

Many parents are convinced that there is a link between food colouring, sugar and caffeine, and children's hyperactive (or manic) behaviour and attempt to cut down on these foods. Although there may be some basis to this, parents who focus exclusively on diet as a cause of their children's restlessness, or inability to concentrate, may miss out on noticing other signs indicating that their child is feeling troubled or uncontained.

## Gender differences and sexual identity

Many parents say that since having a baby they have been convinced that genetic wiring has a greater influence on the way children express their gender identity than they had wished to believe. They may have been full of good intentions to provide an equal playing field and not to encourage a socially imposed role identity on their children. They may have given dolls to their sons, swords to their daughters, but although children of both sexes play with both kinds of toys, left to their own devices, on the whole boys will choose to play with cars and motorbikes, swords and guns, girls will play with tea sets and dolls. Boys will dress up as pirates and cowboys, kings and princes, girls as fairies, princesses and queens. This is a big generalization though, and may be more noticeable in the earlier years. It may have something to do with the fact that boys' gross motor skills in physical coordination for running, jumping and kicking develop earlier than their fine motor skills ability to perform small delicate tasks such as cutting out, and fine drawing and painting. Over time children find outlets in play according to their temperaments. We can never entirely get away from some form of social pressure as children move more into the outside world (or even watch TV). However, it seems important to realize that everyone has a "masculine" and a "feminine" side, regardless of gender. It is a great shame if boys are discouraged from playing at feeding the baby or cooking in the Wendy house because these are "girly" games, or if girls are discouraged from having play fights with swords because those games "are for boys". When little boys dress up in Mummy's shoes and handbags, or girls in Daddy's waistcoat, some parents worry whether their children are confused about their sexual identity, and really wish to be someone of the opposite sex. This is unlikely to be the case. Children try out other identities, expanding on who they are or might become. If children sense parental anxiety they may pick up that this is a taboo area and become secretive. If this early exploration develops into regular cross-dressing, parents may wish to seek advice.

## Tough times

Most small children have to deal with upsetting events of a more or less serious nature. For some children family illness (or their own), separation or divorce, the death of close family members, will be traumatic experiences outside of the normal run of life. If possible, it is helpful to prepare a child for an operation, for example, by taking her to visit the hospital ward where she will be admitted, and showing her, with the aid of simple toys, the sequence of events that will happen to her.

## Telling the truth: when and how much should one tell?

Small children do not have a reliable sense of time and telling them too long in advance about an unpleasant or difficult situation may make them unnecessarily anxious. Adults need time to digest and absorb bad news first, before they talk to a child, otherwise the danger is that their feelings of upset and worry spill out into the child, filling her with distress. Small children need to know the truth about divorce, illness and death, but they do not need to know gory or unnecessarily upsetting details which will haunt and frighten them. If they are not told the truth, or do not get to visit an ill parent in hospital because of fears that this could upset them, their imaginations will work overtime and probably come up with even more frightening fantasy scenarios.

# 6

# Off to Nursery

The transition from his own home to nursery is an exciting but challenging experience for a small child. At home he is familiar with his environment, is more or less the centre of attention, and has his own toys and possessions. At nursery he will be in a new and exciting setting, sharing toys, equipment and the teachers' attention with a large(ish) group of children. There will be many compensations, new toys and activities, space for outdoor play, and the possibility of meeting and playing with a whole range of different children. This can be a frightening prospect too, not all children will be friendly, and the child may miss his mum or dad if things go wrong or at quieter periods of the day, such as mealtimes or nap-times.

Most nurseries have a slow settling-in period over some weeks, so that a child can get used to the staff and environment before a parent leaves. The parent gradually stays away for longer periods until the child can manage the full nursery day. Children often like to bring a special toy or some fruit from home, as these reminders of family life can help them to feel secure in nursery.

## Saying goodbye

It is to be expected that a child may feel upset at saying goodbye to a parent, but with help he will gradually join in with nursery activities, keen to make the most of the new opportunities open to him. However, the moment of parting can be fraught if a child cries and desperately clings onto his mother. He may give the impression that he is "losing her forever" and will never see her again. If he has been badly behaved at home he might feel that she is trying to get rid of him. He might feel that he doesn't get enough time with her, she's always going off to work or the shops and leaving him behind. It is hoped that a child will have had enough good experiences of parents who return to manage the separation and it is helpful if there is a key worker, his "special" person at nursery, someone to comfort him and help him say goodbye.

Sometimes parents decide to "slip out" while their child is busy playing to avoid upsetting their child. The problem with this is that the child suddenly notices that the parent has left without saying goodbye, and can become anxious about when and whether she will return. The child might also find it difficult to concentrate on playing, keeping a watch out for when she might appear or disappear without warning.

In contrast to the clingy upset child, some children run off "from day one without a backward glance", sometimes not even saying goodbye. They simply turn their backs on their parents and are gone, riding off on a trike or busying themselves painting. Although it appears as if they are managing the separation well, this may not be the case. By going off without a proper goodbye, children give the message that separation is too difficult, and that the only way to manage is to turn away, as if they're controlling the separation process. They give the feeling that they are leaving their parents behind rather than the other way around. Managing the pain of separation and saying goodbye properly is an important task which children need help to cope with. If they develop a pattern of avoiding these situations they may have difficulties managing transitions in the future.

It helps if a child knows who will be bringing and collecting him from nursery even if it cannot be the same person each time; the better the child knows the adult, the easier it is all round. Just like at bedtime, a short goodbye ritual can help a child to settle down. Rahana and her mother had a regular ritual of separation each morning at nursery. After hanging her coat and name-tag on her peg, Rahana's mother would sit on a cushion, choose a book and wait for Rahana to climb into her lap. She would read to her until it was time to leave. She would always say, "See you later, alligator", to which Rahana would reply, "In a while, crocodile." They would hug and kiss and Rahana would pat her mum on the head, before she departed.

## Playing out separation issues

Changes and transitions can be painful but are essential for growth and development. When a parent is absent a child has to find a place inside his mind where he can recall a picture of her, to help him manage when she is not physically there. If children are supported and contained by a thoughtful nursery key worker, they can use play to work out these experiences, and slowly learn to put words to their feelings. The use of language in this way helps children develop an ability to think and learn about their experiences and feelings.

David cried bitterly for the first week when his mother left. His cries would follow his mother as far as the gate and she left the building feeling guilty and tearful herself. The key worker decided to take David to a side room on his own for a few minutes each morning after his mother left and offered him some small toy animals to play with. Under the key worker's watchful eye, David began playing with a large elephant and a baby elephant, holding them so the little one had his trunk under the big elephant's tummy. He held them tight so they wouldn't fall apart, then let them go and they fell. Each time they fell he brought them back to their original position. The key worker asked him what he was playing at and he answered, "It is a game about animals who fall", and he looked sadly out of the window as if looking for someone.

It appeared that David was playing out a situation with the "mother" and "baby" elephant, of a parent and child who are together, part from each other, then return back together again. Working this through in the presence of the key worker may have helped David to hold on to a picture in his mind of a mother who returns after she has been away. Over the next week David's cries grew softer as his mother left, and he settled in well.

## Being in a group

Three-year-old children are at a stage when they enjoy being sociable and can get a lot out of group activities and discussion. Water play in the garden or building "junk sculptures" together can be stimulating and rewarding, as long as groups are not too large and are well supervised. As with any group, some children will emerge as leaders, some will be more popular than others; there may be bullying and children who are scapegoated or struggle to fit in. Going to nursery is fun but it can be a strain. At snack-time a newcomer to nursery may not be quick enough to stop the child in the next seat taking a bite out of his biscuit. He may learn to "toughen up" a little, and he may soon be grabbing two biscuits when they come around, to make sure he gets his share in this "tougher" world. But we wouldn't wish for our children to become too used to the idea that the toughest one survives.

It is important for parents to have ongoing regular contact with the nursery staff, to hear how their children are doing and to pick up on or share any concerns before difficulties set in. Sometimes parents hear from their children about an incident of hitting or bullying, and they may be tempted to approach the offending child's parent. It is difficult to resist getting involved when we feel so identified with our children, but sometimes an argument festers on between parents long after the children have forgotten the difficult incident.

## Competitiveness

Three-year-old Pete sat next to Greg at circle time. They were talking about what plants need in order to grow, and the teacher asked what the children had seen growing in their gardens, if they had one. One child said: "I've got a *really* big garden." Pete said, *"I've* got a bigger one *and* we've got ladybirds in ours." The children began shouting out how big their gardens were, the teacher listened a while, then began reading a story about a sunflower.

Rivalry and competition will get going in groups and children often deal with their own envy by making others feel envious, talking about a special toy they have or outing they are going on in a provocative way.

## Imaginary games

Children often play out imaginary games in groups, egging each other on to deeds of bravery, or getting everyone shivering with fear. After circle time, Greg noticed another boy dressing up as a tiger. Greg shouted to Pete, "My God, a tiger! Let's get away!" He tore down to the other side of the room calling to Pete all the while. Other boys gathered and began prodding at the tiger, to get him to attack them. Greg shouted, "The tiger's going to get us!" and crawled under a chair to hide, then came out saying, "Let's run away from the tiger." Greg took some long sticks out of a wooden construction set box and gave some to Pete. The boys began roaring and brandishing their "swords", stamping their feet and looking very excited. Greg said: "These are good for killing the tiger!" The boy in the tiger suit began to back away, looking a little nervous. At this point the nursery worker came in and stood watching, ready to stop the children if their excitement got out of control.

Here we can see how Greg is initiating a game and trying to get Pete to follow his lead. The boys appear to be both frightened by and eager to fight the tiger. Perhaps some of their own fierce or aggressive feelings have been attributed to the tiger, and they wish to triumph over it by killing it.

## Taking a break from the group

Children are usually in a robust mood, ready for the challenge of group activities, but at times they may find it all too much and retreat for a while. The nursery worker Lynn was showing Kim and Tony how to make a snowman. The cardboard body and head had been cut out and the children had to glue them together and cover them with cotton wool. Kim worked in a confident adept way, and had completed the snowman in a few minutes. Tony seemed to be concentrating hard, but was progressing very slowly. He dipped his brush into the glue cautiously and brushed the glue on the shape in circular movements, occasionally stopping to look at Kim's work. He lifted pieces of cotton wool one at a time and very gently pushed them onto the card, then just stood there touching the soft cotton wool and looking into space for several minutes. He seemed to be daydreaming. Perhaps the soft feel of the cotton wool had reminded Tony of mother and home, we can't know, but he had taken himself away from the hurly burly for a break.

## The teacher as parent figure

Parents and nursery teachers are often surprised at how quickly a child can become attached to a particular member of staff. Children need to feel that there are one or two adults with whom they have a close and special relationship and to whom they can turn. They become a bit like a "mummy" in the child's eyes. A child might suddenly become upset and refuse to go to nursery for no apparent reason, until a parent discovers that her favourite teacher is ill or away on holiday, and the puzzle fits together. It can be helpful for parents and children to know well in advance if someone is leaving, as children can become worried by the sudden unexplained disappearance of these important people. Saying goodbye, by having a leaving party or giving a goodbye gift, is an important ritual for the leaver as well as for those left behind, as it is an opportunity to mark an ending, and to acknowledge a sense of separation and loss.

## Rivalry for teacher's attention

One of the biggest challenges for small children coming to nursery is having to share a few adults with so many children. For the child it may feel as if he has suddenly been landed with twenty brothers and sisters and they're all competing for "mummy's" (the teacher's) attention. Much of the behaviour that nursery staff describe as "aggressive" or "violent" in children, such as pushing, kicking or biting, may stem from this difficulty. A child may feel that he has to push or kick his rival "siblings" out of the way, to make sure that the teacher will notice and attend to him.

Those children who have had a good amount of one-to-one attention from a thoughtful parent as babies and toddlers, usually have a reserve of "good mummy feelings" inside them which help them to last a bit longer before demanding attention. These children are also better able to share with others, as they feel less needy than those children who have never had quite enough individual attention when small. These children are still looking for that exclusive parent–child time, which, of course, is difficult to find in a busy nursery. They often end up being sent out of the class, away from the very object they are hoping to get closer to, the teacher, and this can make them feel and behave even worse. The smaller the groups of children, and the higher the ratio of qualified and thoughtful staff available, the better for all concerned.

# Conclusion

Life with a three-year-old is exhilarating and exhausting, full of delights and dramas. By the end of this year children will be launched into nursery school and socializing with friends. They will be self-sufficient in many ways, but will still need the loving care of their parents and close family as they move on to the next adventure, aged four.

# References and Further Reading

Bowlby, J. (1979) *The Making and Breaking of Affectional Bonds*. London: Tavistock.

Bowlby, J. (1988) *A Secure Base: Clinical Applications of Attachment Theory*. London: Routledge.

Harris, M. (1975) *Thinking about Infants and Young Children*. Strath Tay, Perthshire: Clunie Press.

Hindle, D. and Vaciago Smith, M. (eds) (1999) *Personality Development: A Psychoanalytic Perspective*. London: Routledge.

Philips, A. (1999) *Saying "No": Why It's Important for You and Your Child*. London: Faber & Faber.

Rosenbluth, D. with Harris, M., Osborne, E.L. and O'Shaughnessy, E. (1969) *Your 3 Year Old*. London: Corgi.

Waddell, M. (1998) *Inside Lives: Psychoanalysis and the Development of Personality*. Tavistock Clinic Series. London: Duckworth.

Winnicott, D.W. (1964) *The Child, the Family and the Outside World*. London: Penguin.

## Books for your three-year-old child

Ahlberg, A. and Amstutz, A. (1981) *Mrs Lather's Laundry*. Harmondsworth: Puffin.

Ahlberg, J. and Ahlberg, A. (1991) *Each Peach Pear Plum*. London: Viking.

Berenstain, S. and Berenstain, J. (1967) *The Bike Lesson*. London: Collins.

Blake, Q. (1992) *All Join In*. London: Red Fox.

Browne, A. (1995) *Gorilla*. London: Walker.

Carle, E. (1982) *The Bad-tempered Ladybird*. Harmondsworth: Puffin.

Carle, E. (1985) *The Mixed-up Chameleon*. London: Hamish Hamilton.

Carle, E. (1987) *Do You Want to be my Friend?* London: Hamish Hamilton.

Carle, E. (2000) *The Very Hungry Caterpillar*. London: Hamish Hamilton.

Cooper, H. (1995) *Little Monster Did It!* London: Doubleday.

Dickinson, M. (1985) *New Clothes for Alex*. London: Hippo.

Fraiberg, S.H. (1976) *The Magic Years: Understanding the Problems of Early Childhood*. London: Methuen.

French, V. (1995) *Oliver's Vegetables*. London: Hodder.

Garland, S. (1983) *Doing the Washing*. London: Bodley Head.

Garland, S. (1995) *Going Shopping*. London: Puffin.

Hutchins, P. (1994) *You'll Soon Grow into Them, Titch*. London: Red Fox.

McBratney, S. (2001) *I'm Not your Friend*. London: Collins.

McKee, D. (1996) *Not Now, Bernard.* London: Red Fox.

Milne, A.A. (1995) "The End", in *Now We are Six.* London: Methuen.

Milne, A.A. (1973) *Winnie-the-Pooh.* London: Methuen.

Murphy, J. (1995) *Five Minutes' Peace.* London: Magi.

Nicoll, H. and Pieńkowski, J. (1973) *Meg's Eggs.* London: Heinemann.

Oram, H. and Kitamura, S. (1993) *Angry Arthur.* London: Red Fox.

Ross, T. (1986) *I Want my Potty!* London: Andersen.

Sendak, M. (1992) *Where the Wild Things Are.* London: Picture Lions.

Seuss, Dr (2002) *Green Eggs and Ham.* London: HarperCollins.

Waddell, M. and Firth, B. (1988) *Can't You Sleep, Little Bear?* London: Walker.

# Helpful Organizations

**Exploring Parenthood**
Latimer Education Centre
194 Freston Road
London W10 6TT
Tel: 020 8964 1827
Parents' Advice Line: 020 8960 1678
www.globalideasbank.org

**Gingerbread Association for One Parent Families**
7 Sovereign Close
London E1W 2HW
Tel: 020 7488 9300
Advice Line: 0800 018 4318
www.gingerbread.org.uk

**Local SureStart Organisation (in the UK)**
SureStart Unit
DfES and DWP
Level 2, Caxton House
Tothill Street
London SW1H 9NA
Tel: 0870 000 2288
www.surestart.gov.uk

**National Association of Toy and Leisure Libraries**
68 Churchway
London NW1 1LT
Tel: 020 7255 4600
www.natll.org.uk

**Nursery and Pre-school Information Line**
PO Box 5
Brecon LD3 87X
Tel: 01874 638007
www.sutton.lincs.sch.uk

**Parentline Plus**
Tel: 0808 800 2222 (helpline 24 hours a day)
www.parentlineplus.org.uk

**Pre-school Learning Alliance**
61–63 Kings Cross Road
London WC1X 9LL
Tel: 020 7833 0991
www.pre-school.org.uk

**Under-fives Counselling Service**
The Tavistock Clinic
120 Belsize Lane
London NW3 5BA
Tel: 020 7435 7111

**YoungMinds/National Association for Child and Family Mental Health**
102–108 Clerkenwell Road
London EC1M 5SA
Tel: 020 7336 8445
Parents' Information Service: 0800 018 2138
www.youngminds.org.uk

# Index

accident-prone behaviours 23
aggressive behaviours 59–61, 66
  and attention seeking 86
  during play 47–8, 59–60
*All Join In* (Blake) 71
anger 59–66
  coping strategies 66, 70
  and imaginary play 47–8, 59–60
  and nightmares 59, 74
  projecting feelings 28, 50–2, 62
  temper tantrums 61, 62
  verbal expression 24–5
*Angry Arthur* (Oram and Kitamura) 70
anxieties *see* fears

babies 43–4
  build-up to arrival 47–57
  parental decisions 39–41
  preparing older siblings 41–2, 48–9
  responding to questions 42–3
*The Bad-tempered Ladybird* (Carle) 71
bath times 31
bedtimes
  parent's bed 30, 31
  reading stories 70–1
  and relaxation 69–70
  rituals 71
  waking early 49–50
  waking in the night 29–30
  *see also* sleep difficulties
*The Bike Lesson* (Berenstein) 33
birthday parties 55–7
biting 66
Bowlby, John 13
books 33, 77
  bedtime stories 70–1
boundaries 62–4
  *see also* discipline
bribery 64–5
brothers and sisters *see* babies; siblings

bullying behaviours 61
  in group games 83–4

*Can't You Sleep Little Bear?* (Waddell and
  Firth) 71
Christmas, reality and fantasy 22–3
clinging behaviours 81–3
  *see also* separation anxiety
competitiveness 84
conscience and empathy 23–4
  between siblings 46
conversation skills 24–5
copying and mimicking 19–20, 33
cross-dressing 79
curiosity 26

diabetes 78
diet 75–8
  and hyperactivity 78
  junk foods 77–8
  overeating 76
  restricted intakes 77
discipline 23–4
  using bribery 64–5
  different styles 35–6, 62
  saying "no" 62, 63–4
  smacking 65–6
  using threats 64–5
*Do You Want to be my Friend?* (Carle) 71
Dr. Seuss books 77
dreams and nightmares 73–5
  and anger 59
  transference 75
dressing-up
  as coping strategy 22
  and "sameness" 70–1
  and sexual identity 78–9

*Each Peach Pear Plum* (Ahlberg) 71
eating patterns
  food fads 75–7
  junk foods 77–8
  restricted intake 77
empowerment, through play 20–1